Dedicated to the loving memory of

Swamini 'Amma' Saradapriyananda

who attained mahāsamādhī on

April 17, 2000

The Light of Wisdom

THE *Mananam* SERIES

The Light of Wisdom

CHINMAYA PUBLICATIONS
CHINMAYA MISSION WEST PUBLICATIONS DIVISION

Chinmaya Publications
Chinmaya Mission West Publications Division

P.O. Box 129
Piercy, CA 95587, USA

Distribution Office
560 Bridgetowne Pike
Langhorne, PA 19053
Phone: (215) 396-0390   Fax: (215) 396-9710
Toll Free: 1-888-CMW-READ (1-888-269-7323)
Internet: www.chinmayapublications.org

Central Chinmaya Mission Trust
Sandeepany Sadhanalaya
Saki Vihar Road
Mumbai, India 400 072

Credits:

Series Editors: Margaret Leuverink, Rashmi Mehrotra
Consulting Editor: Swami Shantananda
Associate Editor: Neena Dev
Editorial Assistants: Pat Loganathan, Vinni Soni
Text Layout: Arun Mehrotra
Graphics: NMilson Inc. and Arun Mehrotra
Printed by: Central Plains Book Manufacturing

Library of Congress Catalog Card Number 00-111298
ISBN 1-880687-24-0

Swami Satprakashananda. *Vedanta Kesari*. Chennai, India: Vedanta Kesari. Reprinted by permission of Vedanta Kesari Office, Sri Ramakrishna Math, Mylapore, Chennai 6000 004, India.

Swami Vivekananda. *Complete Works of Swami Vivekananda*, v I. Calcutta, India: Advaita Ashram. ©1847, 1971. Reprinted by permission of Advaita Ashram, 5 Dehi Entally Road, Calcutta 14, India.

Swami Vivekananda. *Vedanta Voice of Freedom*. Edited by Swami Chetanananda. St. Louis, Missouri: Vedanta Society of St. Louis. ©1986. Reprinted by permission of Vedanta Society of St. Louis, 205 South Skinker Blvd., St. Louis, Missouri 63105, U.S.A.

Weeraperuma, Susunaga. *The Mountain Path*, Tiruvannamalai, India: Sri Ramanasramam. June, 1996. Reprinted by permission of The Mountain Path, Sri Ramanasramam P.O. Tiruvannamalai, 606 603, India.

Yogananda, Paramahansa. *Autobiography of a Yogi*. Los Angeles, CA: Self-Realization Fellowship. Reprinted by permission of Self-Realization Fellowship, 3880 San Rafael Ave., Los Angeles, California, 90065 USA.

Contents

PART THREE
PEOPLE OF WISDOM

Preface

What is knowledge? What is wisdom? Can these words be used synonymously? At best, some of us tend to think of knowledge as a gathering of information, and wisdom the ability to bring it into practice. We may respect a great scholar, but we have an even greater admiration for those who can act dynamically as the occasion demands, who have sound judgement, and common sense.

In the spiritual traditions these words have a very deep meaning. The Sanskrit word *jnana* (spiritual knowledge) especially has a deep significance. It is often translated as "illumination," as light is used as a synonym for knowledge. Light dispels darkness so also spiritual knowledge dispels ignorance and reveals our true nature. True wisdom is defined as the experience of God and is the topic of "The Light of Wisdom."

In Part One, "Knowledge," the authors help us appreciate the subtle differences between intellectual knowledge and true wisdom. They affirm that it may be possible to get a general knowledge about God through studying the scriptures. But if our goal is true wisdom, we eventually have to leave the words for the actual experience. Just like reading books on physical fitness do not make us fit unless we actually exercise, in the same way intellectual knowledge has to be assimilated before it can be termed as true wisdom. To have this spiritual awakening becomes the topic of Part Two, "The Journey." The authors here show that the real journey is to go within. Constant observation and reflection of one's thoughts and activities in everyday life, along with various spiritual practices, purify the mind so that our lives can become transformed.

The lives of saints and sages are examples of living wisdom. And in Part Three "People of Wisdom" we receive glimpses into the lives of some of these great people. They demonstrate in their lives the divine qualities of wisdom, love, freedom, purity, and joy, and live in the "peace that passeth all understanding."

Thus the crowning glory of human life is to experience God as our Self. We may know much about the objective world, but we can only be truly happy and peaceful when we know and understand the immeasurable treasure that lies within us. The writers in this book urge us not to be satisfied with book knowledge, but to go deeper still in order to perceive the priceless pearl that lies within.

The Editors

PART ONE

Knowledge

He the Sovereign of the Universe
Sustains the tree's stem (the Universe)
In the baseless region
Its branches spread downward
Its roots rest high above.

Ṛg Veda I:24.7

Knowledge is the burning up of ignorance. Ignorance and knowledge are the ascent and descent upon the same ladder. Ignorance is coming down the ladder while knowledge is going up the ladder; the same thing viewed from different standpoints. Science proves that light and darkness are not different, but are one and the same, differing in degree only. Sit in a dark room. After a time the pupil of the eye dilates and you begin to see, and what was darkness becomes light. Knowledge and ignorance are not a pair of opposites. The difference lies in degree, not in kind. As long as you are in ignorance, you are on the lower rungs of the ladder of knowledge.

Swami Ram Tirtha

Men study and pore over books without number in order to know the reality. But the Truth of things is not to be found in the pages of any book; it cannot be attained by just reading about it. It is to be seen and experienced. And the best place to experience it is within oneself. For there one has a direct perception, an intimate feeling which is unmistakable. The divine is in the heart of things and renders himself most accessible at this core. To withdraw the consciousness from its preoccupations in a hundred directions outside and center it within oneself is the surest way to become aware of the Truth stationed within and to realize it.

M.P. Pandit

I

The Two Kinds of Knowledge

by Swami Ranganathananda

In the opening passage of the seventh chapter of the *Chāndogya Upaniṣad* we see a highly educated student, Narada, approaching a great spiritual teacher, Sanatkumara and confessing to him: "O Blessed One! I am full of sorrow (in spite of all my intellectual knowledge); and I have heard from great teachers like you that only he who knows his own Infinite Self, and no one else, can cross over sorrow. O Blessed One! please take me across this ocean of sorrow."

Sanatkumara replies: "Please tell me what you already know."

Narada then lists all the subjects that he has studied so far. The list is extensive, it includes the Vedas, history, and many other sources of knowledge. But the teacher remarks, "Yes, you know much, but they are all mere words, words, words!"

Education has to go beyond words to meaning, beyond knowledge to wisdom. Western thinkers who come across these new inspiring ideas in Vedanta and yoga are now trying to understand man from a deeper dimension. All the current education and even the Freudian view of man are still only surface views compared to the in-depth study of man in Indian thought. It seems, particularly in the West, that the more educated the person, the more complex and disintegrated his mind. Simple minds are better than disintegrated complex minds. The educated person of today is merely strong intellectually.

Even the late Bertrand Russell, a brilliant intellectual and an agnostic, said, "Unless men increase in wisdom as much as in knowledge, increase of knowledge will be increase of sorrow."[1] What a beautiful idea! Bertrand Russell was merely echoing the deeply felt urges of the modern man of today but he could not explain the meaning of wisdom. When we turn to the Upanishads, however, we find the same beautiful idea expressed in the same language, and it is there that we can discover the true meaning of "wisdom."

Indian tradition upholds that there are two types of knowledge: One is knowledge, the other is matured knowledge, when knowledge becomes wisdom. Science or knowledge is called *vidyā* in Sanskrit. The first chapter of the *Muṇḍaka Upaniṣad* contains the following anecdote: A student goes to a teacher and asks him: "What is that (truth), O Blessed One! by knowing which one can know everything in this manifested universe?" (I:1.3) Everything that we experience in this manifested universe we experience as an object, including the body, the sense organs, the sun, moon, and stars. The question is really an inquiry into the One behind the many.

The teacher gives a beautiful answer: "Two kinds of science or knowledge are to be inquired into by man, so say the sages who know the truth of the ultimate Reality or *Brahman*: one is called *aparā vidyā*, ordinary knowledge; the other is called *parā vidyā*, higher knowledge." (I:1.4)

Both are sciences, but the first deals with the world of change, the *loka*, that is, the reality as revealed by the five senses and by instruments helpful to the senses. The other deals with the changeless, *lokottara*, that is, the reality that is transcendental, eternal, and that lies beyond the reach of the senses and the sense-bound mind. The teacher means to say that all the sacred books in the world like the Vedas, the Koran, the Bible, and astronomy as well as other sciences, linguistics, grammar, and so on — in fact, all positivistic knowledge — belong to the category of *aparā vidyā*.

The teacher of the Upanishad is detached, scientific, and bold. He includes even the Vedas into this category, in spite of the high esteem in which these sacred books are held by every-one in the country. What boldness, arising from single-minded love for truth and scientific detachment, we find in the thinking of these sages of the Upanishads! In no other religious tradition will we find this kind of scientific temper and courage. One's own sacred book is always considered to be the highest to the followers of any religion, but not so to these Hindu sages. To them even the sacred books are ordinary knowledge, *aparā vidyā*. That this scientific temper is an ancient tradition in India is verified by what Shri Ramakrishna says in our own time. In the Vedas and other scriptures, you do not get God, but only in-formation about God; they are just like the Hindu calendar, which often contains a forecast of the rainfall of the year — this year, there will be so many centimeters of rainfall. But, says, Shri Ramakrishna, if you squeeze the pages, you won't get a single drop of water!

In the same way, if you squeeze the Vedas or other sacred books, you won't get that imperishable Reality, that *parā vidyā* or wisdom. The teacher in the Upanishad defines it as follows: "That by which that imperishable Reality can be realized," and which we can only get by "squeezing our own self." Man is thus his own greatest mystery. He does not understand the vast veiled universe into which he has been cast because he does not under-stand himself. He comprehends but little of his organic pro-cesses, and even of his unique capacity to perceive the world about him, to reason and to dream. Least of all does he under-stand his noblest and most mysterious faculty: the ability to tran-scend himself and perceive himself in the act of perception.

Knowing is Being

Swami Vivekananda has given expression to his ideas on educa-tion lucidly and comprehensively. How could Swamiji speak with such irresistible appeal on education? The answer lies in his own experience of education and its comprehensive nature.

While in school and college, he had studied the modern sciences, history, and literature with keen interest. Earlier he had imbibed at his mother's feet the spiritual and cultural traditions of his own ancient country. But his education was not yet complete. This "educated" Narendra had to go and sit at the feet of an "uneducated" man — the great Shri Ramakrishna (1836-1886) for five years, to complete his education and emerge as Swami Vivekananda! What a strange spectacle is this anecdote in the modern age! Not only he, but also other highly educated and intellectual youths had to approach the "uneducated" Shri Ramakrishna living in Dakshineswar, north of Calcutta, to continue and complete their education.

But who was this Shri Ramakrishna? He had never gone to school beyond the first or second year of the primary level. He was just ordinary; and yet he was also something extraordinary; for he had given himself an education in what I had referred to earlier as the *parā vidyā* of the *Muṇḍaka Upaniṣad* and it was those teachings that had found their fulfillment in him. Narendra and the other young disciples represented *aparā vidyā*, while Shri Ramakrishna represented *parā vidyā*. And the modern age experienced again, what ancient India had always upheld, the extraordinary spectacle of *aparā vidyā* going to *parā vidyā* to fulfil itself. This confirmed three truths to which the Indian tradition has always held fast during the several millennia of her history.

1. *Aparā vidyā* must rise to the level of *parā vidyā* to fulfil itself — knowledge must rise to wisdom.

2. There is an unbroken continuity in human education from *aparā vidyā* to *parā vidyā*.

3. *Parā vidyā* and *aparā vidyā* are complementary and never contradictory.

Physical science and all the rest deal only with things that change, that are perishable. As Sir Arthur Eddington said, science gives us "knowledge of structural form and not knowledge of content." Again in the words of Shri Ramakrishna, "In the sacred books you do not get God, but only information about God." And yet we feel that, in the words of Eddington, "All through the physical universe runs that unknown content."

What is that content? And how can we get at it? If the positive sciences cannot get at it, there must be another discipline another line of inquiry, which must be able to give us that truth. If the sacred books contain only information about God, there must be a discipline that gives us God and not merely information about Him. It is this inquiry that pervades the Upanishads and that has made them immortal even as literature. And the nature and scope of that inquiry, the way it was conducted, and the truths gained from them have something superb about them. There is no effort to uphold a mere opinion, however dear; no struggle to pronounce a dogma and cling to it, and thrust it upon others; there is no trace of tiredness, or laziness of mind, seeking a resting place on the way. Truth, and nothing but truth, is the watchword.

This kind of boldness arising from love of truth, which we saw in Shri Ramakrishna in our own time, was there in the philosophical and religious tradition of India from the time of the Vedas and the Upanishad. The Vedas themselves declare: "To the knower of Truth, the Vedas become irrelevant." In the *Bhagavad Gītā* Lord Krishna similarly exhorts Arjuna: "The Vedas deal with the three *guṇa*. O Arjuna! you go beyond them." (II.45).

We transcend the scriptures, with their do's and don'ts, and all these static traditions, when we experience the truth for ourselves. Knowledge rising to wisdom is only when we begin to experience the profound truth about ourselves. The way that Vedanta conveys this truth can be summed up in one sentence: In all scientific investigations into the inner dimension of man, which is also the inner dimension of nature (for man is nature's finest product of evolution) every knowing tends to be being. To know *it,* is to be *it.* In no other physical science is this true. If we know the table, we don't become the table; when we know the sun, we don't become the sun. But in the science of the inner nature of man, when we know the *Ātman*, we become the *Ātman*, when we know God, we become God, or become God-like. What a beautiful idea! There we find speculative knowledge becoming experiential knowledge. This is what Vedanta calls knowledge maturing into wisdom.

In many Upanishads we come across the question: Is there anything permanent in this world of change? And we see the way in which the sages investigated and answered this question. In modern Western thought we also come across this question, as all science is really the search for the imperishable behind the perishable. Everything in the universe is perishable, including our own bodies. Vedanta says that only through the pursuit of Truth into the deepest level of experience, will we get the imperishable and the immortal. Then we realize ourselves not as a body, but as the immortal and we exclaim, "I am the infinite *Ātman*. I am the Self; I am Shiva!" That wonderful knowledge is not second-hand knowledge but direct experience. Here knowledge becomes experience. "There is the *Ātman* in me" is only information. But "I am the *Ātman*" is an experience; and experience at the level of *parā vidyā* or trans-sensory knowledge level is what makes for wisdom.

FOOTNOTE

[1]   Impact of Science on Society, p. 121

II

The Purpose of Knowledge

by Swami Tejomayananda

The words *education* and *knowledge* have a general meaning and also a special meaning as indicated in the scriptures. Here I would like to explain the words from a spiritual point of view. We generally understand education to mean schooling, and we say, "We are giving our children the best education." We do not say, "We are giving them the best knowledge." Our educational system can provide data and information, but it does not give students a direction and a higher goal to strive for. And when there is no ideal, there is no further progress or development of character. Thus education prepares us to live only one aspect of life but it does not really help us to discover the truth of life itself. Knowledge, on the other hand, prepares us to face life squarely and brings about a transformation within ourselves. Therefore the purpose of true education is to lead a person to that knowledge by which he can discover the truth for himself.

Shankaracharya gave the purpose of knowledge in one very precise statement. He said that *the result of knowledge is the elimination of falsehood*. This implies that if we understand something as false, we withdraw ourselves from it. When our understanding changes our wrong behavior also ends. The following example will illustrate this: While walking on the road, a man saw a small glittering object. Thinking that it was a precious piece of silver he picked it up. On further inspection, however, he realized that it was only a piece of rock wrapped in silver paper. Thinking that it was silver, he had picked it up, but the moment that he discovered that it was not silver (true knowledge) he threw the rock away (false concept was eliminated). He will now forget all about the incident and will never mention it to anyone because no one likes to talk about his mistakes. This shows that when real knowledge takes place there will also be humility, because after a person discovers the truth, he simply realizes how foolish he has been.

Thus the true purpose of knowledge is to eliminate all false notions. Up until now we have based our lives upon certain concepts, many of which are false, and therefore the activity arising from them is also false. Some of those false concepts are that we are the body, or that money gives us security, or that all pleasures derived through our sense organs can make us truly happy. When we awaken to true Knowledge, however, all of our sufferings come to an end, and this Knowledge in Sanskrit is called *jñāna*.

Classifying Knowledge

The *Bhagavad Gītā* classifies knowledge according to three different visions, technically termed as *sāttvika jñāna*, *rājasika jñāna* and *tāmasika jñāna*. *Sāttvika jñāna* is the highest knowledge, and *tāmasika jñāna* is the lowest. What then is this true Knowledge, the highest Knowledge?

Our gross and subtle bodies are the medium through which we contact the outer world. When we look through them we see the variety and duality of this world; this is their function. But while seeing this variety, if we are able to see the one Reality pervading all these differences — to recognize the One in the many — this is called the highest Knowledge.

Our physical body is a good example of this idea. We see that there are many different parts — the hands, the fingers, the stomach, the head, and the legs — but even though the parts are many, we know that this entire body is *me*. We do understand the concept of the oneness in regards to the body and that is why, if somebody touches our back, we will not say, "Why are you touching *my back?*" We will say, "Why are you touching *me?*" As one entity, I am pervading all the parts. The highest Knowledge, or *sāttvika jñāna* then, is to be able to see the one Reality that pervades through all the names and forms of the universe.

The lower or *rājasika* knowledge sees and understands each thing as being distinct and separate from every other object. For example, an optometrist studies only the eyes and a painter notices only color and form. Most of us do not see the world as a whole or in totality but consider all things to be separate and unrelated to each other. That is why we say *my* house, *my* share, *your* share, and so on. Though the Lord has created only one earth and space, the world has divided it into nations, countries, and even different national "air spaces!" This is called *rājasika* knowledge.

The lowest knowledge is called *tāmasika jñāna*. This is where one takes a certain part of the whole and gets very attached to that one object, view, or belief. For example, the feeling that my path alone is right, yours is wrong, my religion is right, yours is wrong. This is the lowest vision or attitude toward life. The person with *tāmasika* knowledge is intolerant and fanatical, and the person who thinks so narrowly will always be agitated. On the other hand, if one has the vision of oneness, if one has *sāttvika jñāna*, one's attitude and behavior will be extremely noble and peaceful.

Love and Service to All

The same attitude that we have towards our physical body can also be applied to higher Knowledge. Suppose, while talking, my finger accidentally pokes my eye. Will I not use the very same finger to rub my eye and console it? I will not cut off the finger and throw it away because it has hurt my eye. Similarly, if the teeth accidentally bite the tongue we do not break the teeth in order to punish them. I have no hatred towards my teeth and no desire to hurt them because the teeth are also a part of myself and are just as dear to me as every other part of the body. Thus we see that where there is a sense of oneness we are raised immediately to an attitude of *love* for everything. When there is love for all, service to all automatically manifests.

Today we are not able to serve, not because there is no love, but because the sense of oneness is not there. This vision of oneness is called true Knowledge or Wisdom. Throughout our formal education, we must be led to this highest Knowledge, which will bring about a transformation within ourselves. If one person changes, he can change the world around him. Although there have been few saints and sages, yet each of them has had a great influence upon many people. The wise man hates none and is a friend to all. When that vision of oneness comes, our lives will be totally changed. Do not wait for others to change, begin with yourself. You are the world and the world is not different from you. Change your attitude, and your vision of the world will change. Everything will be peaceful and good. This is the non-dualism of Vedanta. This is the highest Knowledge and true Wisdom.

III

Krishnamurti and the Direct Perception of Truth

by Professor P. Krishna

Krishnamurti was one of the most original thinkers of our time who investigated fundamental questions about the purpose of life, the true meaning of love, religion, time and death without seeking answers in any books or scriptures and without accepting any belief, organized religion or system of thought. Like the Buddha, he sought the answers to these questions through observation, inquiry and self-knowledge and arrived at a direct perception of truth, which lies beyond intellectual concepts, theories, and descriptions. He was not a scholar or an intellectual; he did not deal with theories and concepts, he spoke only from his own investigations and observations. What he has said may have been said earlier by others but he came upon the truth of it for himself. In an age dominated by science and the intellect, he has pointed out the fundamental limitations of thought and knowledge as a means of real change. In this article I propose to reflect on some of the essential aspects of his teaching and some of the great truths he has expounded.

The Source of All Human Problems

Over the million years or more that man has existed on this planet his knowledge of the external world has evolved greatly and increased his power over it. Inwardly, in his consciousness, man has not evolved very much. Psychologically he is still very much like the primitive man — fearful and insecure, forming groups (religious and national), fighting and preparing for war, seeking advantages for himself and hating others. He is now able to travel to the moon and communicate around the globe in a matter of minutes but he still finds it difficult to love his neighbor and live in peace. Modern man is as brutal, selfish, violent, greedy and possessive as the primitive man of a million years ago, though he may now be able to hide himself behind a lot of noble-sounding words and thoughts. This lopsided development of the human being has brought him close to self-annihilation. He stands now on the brink of nuclear war, just a hair's breadth away from total extinction. The power that his increased knowledge has given him has not been coupled with the right kind of intelligence and vision that are necessary. Why? Why have we not evolved psychologically? Is it because we have never directed our attention inwards to understand our own mind, thoughts, and feelings? We are so satisfied, so dazzled by our achievements, our "progress" in the outer world, that we have completely neglected the inner world of our consciousness. Hatred in the primitive man could do only little damage; in modern man with all his power it is much more devastating and we see it every day all around us.

It seems to us that we can resolve this problem if we can organize things better in society. This is a deep-rooted illusion. One is, of course, not against efficient organization of daily life, but you cannot produce a non-violent and peaceful society with a million violent aggressive, self-seeking individuals, in whatever manner you may organize them. If you have a communist society, you will have the violence of the communist ideology; if you have a capitalist society, you will have the violence of the capitalist ideology. If you contain the violence in some areas, it will erupt in others. Revolutions have come and gone but man's tyranny over man has not ended — it has only assumed other forms.

A truly peaceful, non-violent society is only possible if the individual is transformed psychologically, fundamentally. Any other change is trivial, temporary — it will never resolve the problems; it will only enable us to cope with them for a while. Society is what the individual is. Just as the characteristics of a bar of copper are determined by the characteristics of the atoms constituting it, the characteristics of a society are determined by those of its individuals. All the problems that we see in society today are reflections of the problems in the psyche of the individual. Therefore we must concern ourselves with the inner transformation of man and not just the outer organization of society.

Changing the Individual

All religions have tried to change man, but they have failed. Had they succeeded, we would not have so much cruelty, war, and hatred today. We must examine why religions have failed to change man and learn from this. Essentially, every religion has prescribed a path, a set of virtues to be practiced and vices to be eschewed. And man has struggled for thousands of years to do what they prescribe, but it has not worked. The practice of virtuous acts does not in itself alter the consciousness of man. The practice of pre-meditated acts of kindness does not produce kindness in one's consciousness. It becomes another achievement, another aim in life, another method of seeking self-satisfaction. On the other hand, if there is kindness in the heart, it will express itself in every action, every thought, word and deed. Then it does not have to be "practiced." Similarly, one cannot practice nonviolence as long as one is aggressive, hateful, and violent inwardly. Then non-violence becomes only a facade, a hypocritical exterior, and a cold calculated performance. It is only by observing the causes of violence in oneself and eliminating them (not through effort but through understanding) that there can be an ending of violence. And when there is the ending of violence, there is no need to practice non-violence. Only a lazy mind needs to discipline itself!

So, virtue cannot be practiced; it cannot be cultivated. It is a state of mind, a state of consciousness, which arises when there is self-knowledge, understanding, clarity and vision. It cannot be achieved through willful effort, it requires insight. And insight comes through observation, through reflection, through sensitive awareness. It is the perception of truth that liberates consciousness from its ignorance and illusions; and it is ignorance that generates disorder in the psyche. Goodness must be spontaneous; otherwise it is not goodness. Any change in the outward conduct of man brought about through fear, coercion, discipline, conformity, imitation or propaganda does not represent a true change in consciousness and is therefore both superficial and contradictory.

The Importance of Self-Inquiry

From time immemorial man has depended on a guru, a religion or a book to show him the way. Krishnamurti has pointed out that truth is a pathless land and no guru, no path, no belief, no book can lead you to it. You have to be a light unto yourself and not seek light from another. The role of the guru is only to point out; it is the individual himself who has to learn. And the ability to learn is far more important than the ability to teach. In this field, no one can really teach anything to anyone else. Each one has to come upon the truth for oneself, and one must begin with knowing oneself. Without understanding the workings of one's own thought-processes and the conditioning one has acquired from one's own experiences, tradition, culture, religion and so on, one cannot find the true answer to any serious question. Our beliefs, our opinions, conclusions and prejudices prevent us from seeing things in their true perspective because they color our vision. One must be aware of this fact and doubt every opinion; every conclusion that comes to the mind for it may not represent the truth. When one inquires into oneself in that way, with the intention of seeking the truth and not merely seeking satisfaction, learning takes place. And one must live with that state of inquiry, questioning and doubting, without seeking to arrive.

What one can receive from another is a thought, a question; but the exploration has to be one's own. Unless you come upon the truth for yourself it is not the truth for you — it is only a description of the truth. That is the difference between the Buddha and the Professor of Buddhist philosophy. The former has the actual insight, the consciousness; the latter has only a description of it.

Man has often confused the symbol, the word, or the concept for the real thing. A true Christian is one who lives by *The Sermon on the Mount* (and you can only do that if you have the consciousness of Christ), not the man who joins a church and performs all its rituals. A true Buddhist is one who partakes of the consciousness of the Buddha, not one who obeys the Buddhist church. All churches, all organized religions have only succeeded in reducing the great truth to a mere system, a symbol, a ritual. What matters are not the garment, the label, but the content of the consciousness within.

The role of a teacher (the guru) is that of the lamp on the roadside. One must not sit and worship the lamp; one must walk the way. Krishnamurti repeatedly emphasized that it had very little significance if we either accepted or rejected what he said. It is only when we consider it, question it, examine it, and discover for ourselves if it is true or not that it has value. Since truth and liberation are something the individual has to come upon by himself, through his own inquiry, any organization that tries to propagate "truth" through belief, conformity or propaganda only serves to further condition the mind of the individual and enslave him. A meaningful inquiry requires freedom from all belief, prejudices, conclusions and conditioning. It requires a deep awareness of oneself as one is. Since truth cannot be organized and spread, spiritual organizations which try to do this have no value.

The Limitations of Intellectual Understanding

We are often satisfied with an intellectual answer to a question and that puts an end to our inquiry. When that happens, intellectual understanding is a hindrance to the discovery of the truth. It is easy to see intellectually that one must not worry when one's child is ill. The worrying does not help the child. What helps him is our fetching a doctor and giving the patient the medicine. Of course we do that, but does this logical conclusion prevent us from worrying? Does the knowledge that anger is evil prevent anger? The truth is much deeper than mere logic and reason; and the intellectual answer is not a complete answer. So, when one has understood something only intellectually one has understood but little. Intellectual understanding may be useful in some matters but it is trivial. It can be secured through a book or through another but is only a thought-pattern held in memory; it should not be mistaken for the realization of the truth of something.

So if intellectual understanding is a limited thing, then what reveals the truth? For this, one must observe oneself and one's thought process like a true scientist observes a phenomenon in which he is interested. He doesn't want to change it: he observes it without choice, without letting his own desires interfere with his observation. When one observes oneself in that way, with choice-less and passive awareness, without a desire to quickly form an opinion or come to a conclusion, patiently and with skepticism, for the sake of understanding oneself and life, only then can one discover what is true and what is false. Then the false drops away by itself without any effort of will. Ignorance then dissolves in the light of understanding. Without such an objective and yet passionate investigation of oneself, of all one's conclusions, beliefs, attachments, desires and motivations, it has very little meaning to intellectually identify oneself with some group, some theory, some belief and plead for it like a lawyer for the rest of one's life. It is as absurd as saying, "My country is the best country because I was born in it." Yet, that is what nationalism implies.

It is the tragedy of our life that we are never educated to look at ourselves in the right manner. We are only educated to learn about the external world and to somehow cope with its problems. Therefore one grows up knowing so much about the external world and yet being totally ignorant of oneself, one's desires, ambitions, values and outlook on life. We may be very skilled at our jobs but we are totally confused about whether pleasure brings happiness, whether desire and attachment are the same thing as love, and why differences between men turn into inequalities. Happiness, love, nonviolence, and humility are not something one can work for directly. They come as a by-product of inquiry, self-knowledge and understanding, which inwardly cleanse our consciousness without imposing on it any fixed opinions, beliefs or patterns of thought. If one sees very clearly through close and careful examination that the pursuit of pleasure does not lead to happiness, then one's outlook towards pleasure in life alters at the source and the pursuit of pleasure drops away without any effort, sacrifice, or suppression. Then there is a natural austerity, which is totally different from the self-imposed practice of austerities.

Similarly if one actually realized, through one's own observation and investigation, that one is not essentially different from other human beings because one shares with them the same problems — of fear, insecurity, desire, greed, violence, loneliness, sorrow, self-interest — then one would approach the state of oneness with others. Through our ignorance we give tremendous importance to the relatively superficial differences between us, like the differences in belief, in prosperity, in knowledge, in ability, which are all only acquisitions. We have not asked ourselves why we give such tremendous importance to our acquisitions, why we let them divide us from others when in reality we share the same human consciousness. If you mentally strip a man of all his wealth, possessions, status, beliefs and knowledge and look into his consciousness, is it really very different from that of any other human being? Just as the caste, color, or creed of a human being does not change the composition of his blood, all our acquisitions, whether mental or material, do not alter the content of our consciousness. If we do not prevent ourselves from seeking the truth of this, we will actually realize the underlying unity of humanity. It is ignorance that divides us, not the differences between us.

Mankind is caught in a great illusion. It thinks it can solve its problems through legislation, through political and social reform, through scientific and technological progress, through greater knowledge, greater wealth, greater power, and greater control. It may solve some problems with all this; but they are all trivial problems and temporary palliatives. They will have the effect of aspirin but they will not cure the disease. We shall go on creating new problems on the one hand, and trying to solve them on the other in order to maintain the illusion of "progress." And not much time is left now, for the disease is growing at a wild pace and is about to consume us. If man does not transform himself inwardly, through conscious redirection of his psyche, he will soon join the list of those predecessors who lived a million years or so on this planet and then became extinct for they could not adapt themselves. It is not certain yet if the evolution of man from the monkey was really a step in the direction of survival or a retrograde step. Only time will tell.

IV

Divine Inspiration

by Swami Abhedananda

The God of tradition is not the real God, and the God of rhetoric is not the absolute Spirit, but when we have broken these ideals of a man-made God, then the infinite Spirit fires our hearts with divine presence and inspires our souls with Divine wisdom and love.

The God of Vedanta is like a circle whose circumference is nowhere, but whose center is everywhere. Each of these centers is an individual soul or ego, and that circle is the universal spirit. The center lies in each one of us, but the circle is overhead and all around us. This unlimited circle is the source of infinite wisdom and love. All the blessed qualities proceed from it, because it forms the background of all individual souls. At present we do not know how wise and good we are in reality. We are living like fools searching here and there for a ray of the light of wisdom, which is shining in its own glory behind our mind, intellect, and heart. It takes a long time to discover the light of wisdom that lies behind the veil of the clouds of egotism and selfishness. These clouds hide the face of the sun, and so we cannot see it.

In the majority of people, the clouds of egotism and selfishness are thick and dark, and therefore they grope in the darkness of ignorance without perceiving a ray of immortal light. They mistake the transitory objects of the senses for the reality. They live on the sense-plane, and mistake the body for the soul and matter for spirit.

Blessed are those whose clouds of egotism and selfishness have become thin and transparent. They can see and bathe in the sunshine of the infinite wisdom. They are the great teachers of the world, but their number is few and far between. God, the Divine Being, shines through their souls and speaks through their mouths the message of the absolute Truth. They are the Christs and Buddhas; they are the Krishnas and Ramakrishnas; they are the inspired Prophets of this world. They do not fill their minds with second or third-hand knowledge, which comes filtered through the imperfect brains of ordinary mortals. They go to the fountainhead of all wisdom and from there bring new light into the world. They teach from within. Their teachings are full of inspiration and revelation, and not like the teachings of ordinary thinkers. They do not pass their opinions like the surface scientists and ignorant philosophers, who do not really teach, but give their opinions, making their imperfect intellect the standard of truth and thus they delude the minds of the masses. The opinions of ordinary teachers are nothing but the expressions of partial knowledge or imperfect understanding, but the teachings of the inspired ones last throughout eternity. They are always the same, because truth is eternal.

Eternal Wisdom

Much of the wisdom that we find in this world is not real wisdom. The knowledge of today will become the ignorance of tomorrow. We shall have to throw it out, but real wisdom does not change; it is unchangeable and immutable. The unchangeable eternal wisdom is the infinite Being. Those who follow the teachings of the supreme mind, receive the true wisdom that lies in it. No one except the supreme mind can teach the lower mind; no one besides the Universal Spirit can teach the individual soul. Ordinary mortals may pass their opinions, and these opinions may appeal to us for the time being, but they never go deep into the bottom of our soul being. They touch only the surface of our soul and there they end. But the real truth, when it begins to manifest or shine, penetrates the bottom of our souls and enters into the core of the hearts of the beings.

There is an old proverb that says, "God comes to see us without a bell." That is, God comes in silence and inspires us when our minds are not disturbed by the cares and anxieties of the phenomenal world. If you want to hear the voice of the Supreme God who speaks within, you will have to go into your room and close the door, as Jesus Christ said. Here "the room" does not mean an external room, but it means the room of our hearts, and "the door" does not mean the outside door of a room, but it means the door of the senses. When the senses are silent and the mind and intellect are still, then the Lord comes, pays us a visit, and whispers into the heart.

There is another saying: "Let us be silent, for so are the gods." The silence of the senses, and the mind and intellect is the only condition in which we receive divine inspiration, but this silence does not come until we have gone through many intermediate stages of evolution. These stages are indicated by the struggles of our mind and intellect. First of all, we must search after the Truth by exercising our mental and intellectual powers. We cannot realize God until we have exhausted the resources which we possess. We first try to know God by exercising our intellect. We go here and there and ask many questions seeking the help of external teachers. At this stage intellectual perception appeals to us, but later on we find that the intellect cannot reveal the absolute Truth.

Through all these struggles, however, we arrive at a point where we find that our intellect fails to reveal the eternal Truth, yet we are still progressing all the time. These struggles are only the outward signs of the progress of the soul. The progress of the soul really comes from within. It is the gradual unfoldment of the latent powers and wisdom. As the bud of a lotus gradually unfolds its petals by a power which is not outside, but within it, so the bud of the individual soul gradually unfolds the powers and wisdom which are already there by going through different stages of mental and intellectual evolution. These are necessary for spiritual progress. Mental and intellectual evolutions gradually bring out the wisdom of the soul, which is pure consciousness and feeling.

We cannot know what powers we possess unless they are brought out on the plane of our knowledge. As long as they are latent on the subconscious plane, we do not feel that we possess them, but, when we are conscious of them, they are ours and become our property. And this knowledge or consciousness comes through the process of evolution or unfoldment. No one can teach us, but we teach ourselves. The external teachers only give us suggestions, and whatever appeals to our souls we receive, and the rest we reject.

Listening to the Inner Voice

Such suggestions from the outside teachers are necessary as long as we have not been able to discover the suggestions from within, from the higher Self. The higher Self is constantly giving us suggestions, but we remain deaf to them and so cannot catch and appreciate them. When, however, we have begun to hear the inner voice, we do not need any external teacher, and then we get lessons directly from the Divine Being, and that is called "divine inspiration." In divine inspiration, we receive lessons directly from God. There we come face to face with the Supreme Being and enter into close communion with the omniscient Spirit. Whoever has received such divine inspiration does not need any outside teacher. But we must not forget to hear the inner voice which comes all the time from the higher Self, and we must make our minds and the senses silent to receive that voice. It is the same as if we want to learn something from an external teacher, we also must make our minds receptive and listen intently. So if we wish to hear the voice of the divine teacher within us, we must make our minds receptive and turn our full attention toward the higher Self. We must not let our minds be distracted by the external objects of the senses, but must watch intently how the voice comes, and then catch it quickly.

But how is it possible for us to hear the voice of the Lord, when our minds are filled with the impurities of cares and anxieties and all the temporal phenomenal thoughts and things with which we are absorbed at present? The moment that we try to hear the voice of the Lord within us our minds are distracted by the sounds and thoughts of transitory things. Therefore, we cannot hear it. Our power of hearing is not developed, because we are constantly fixing our attention on the objects of the senses. We think that these senses are the only gates of knowledge and inspiration, but in reality, they are not, they only bring partial knowledge. But if we observe closely, we find that we do not receive any knowledge from outside. All knowledge proceeds from within. The sense objects will never give us an iota of knowledge, if the knowledge is not there within our soul. The sense objects will never reveal anything to us as we perceive the objects of the senses. And it should be remembered that when we seek knowledge from the external world, we put the cart before the horse through ignorance. We should turn our eyes beyond the sense and should see the source from where the senses draw their power or driving force.

The river of knowledge is constantly flowing in our soul, but we do not know where that river is flowing. The source is beyond our sight and also beyond our intellectual perception. In the darkness of ignorance, we think that the source is outside of us on the sense plane. And so we analyze the material particles in order to get some revelation, but we forget that the material particles do not possess wisdom and that it is the soul that possesses true wisdom. And on account of this ignorance, we waste a great deal of our time and energy.

The knowledge is our property by birthright. No one can

deprive us of that knowledge. We must not forget, however that we are our own friends when we look within and search within, but we become our own enemies when, neglecting our true Self, we go outside in search after knowledge. Book learning will never teach us and never bring the truth, but true knowledge will come from the soul. We may read all the books that exist in the world, but our thirst for knowledge will not be quenched by the book learning. We need the inspiration of higher Spirit within us in order to quench that thirst. When we leave aside all books and sit in silence, searching after that knowledge of the Supreme Spirit, then we are more learned than all the books can make us. If we sit for half an hour in silence, we will learn more than by readings thousands and thousands of volumes. It is in silence that God speaks within us. In that state, the higher Soul reveals its true nature and the veil that has covered its face, is then lifted up. That is the meaning of "revelation" or "flash of Divine Knowledge."

PART TWO

The Journey

*I, the devotee am standing
In the midst of deep water,
Yet I feel thirsty, O blissful Lord,
Have mercy, slake my thirst,
and bless me with happiness and contentment*

Ṛg Veda VII:89.4

The way to realize God is through discrimination, renunciation, and yearning for Him. What kind of yearning? One should yearn for God as the cow, with a yearning heart, runs after its calf. Add tears to your yearning. And if you can renounce everything through discrimination and dispassion then you will be able to see God. That yearning brings about God-intoxication whether you follow the path of knowledge or the path of devotion.

Shri Ramakrishna
The Gospel

The truth of the Self is extremely subtle and cannot be reached by a distracted mind. It is realized only by noble souls of pure mind, and even by them only through extraordinary concentration. . . . In order that the Knowledge of *Brahman* may be realized directly and clearly, "like a fruit on the palm of one's hand," and not merely understood intellectually, Vedanta prescribes certain disciplines, known as hearing *śravanam*, reflecting *mananam*, meditating *nididhyāsanam*, and absorption in *Brahman* or *samādhī*.

Swami Nikhilananda

Self-Knowledge

V

Service and Self-Knowledge

by Swami Chidananda
(Chinmaya Mission)

Self-knowledge is indeed the supreme goal of life. In Self-knowledge alone there is complete cessation of sorrow and the attainment of Supreme Bliss. Therefore, it is important to know the relation of "service" or selfless work to Self-knowledge. Right at the beginning of his commentary while introducing the *Bhagavad Gītā*, Shri Shankara gives us a broad picture of the teachings of the Vedas. Two-fold is the *dharma* taught by the Vedas consisting of *pravṛtti* (engaging oneself in work, dynamic action) and *nivṛtti* (withdrawal from work, into a contemplative life). Prosperity in the world (*abhyudaya*) is the result of *pravṛtti*, while knowledge and dispassion characterize *nivṛtti*. A life of serene contemplation on Vedanta requires a mind that is highly pure and mature. An extrovert mind attached to sense objects cannot appreciate and realize the Supreme Knowledge or *Brahma-vidyā*. To such a mind, *nivṛtti* and hence Self-knowledge are impossible. Therefore, there arises the practical question of how one may evolve and become fit for the pursuit of Self-knowledge. The answer to this very question is *karma-yoga* otherwise called as selfless service, *yajña-karma*, *sevā*, *niṣkāma karma* and so on.

For the overwhelming majority of us, action is unavoidable. Our nature forces us to work even if we go to an ashram or to the Himalayas. In the *Bhagavad Gītā*, Lord Krishna says to Arjuna,

"Your nature will make you act and prevent you from withdrawing to any quiet life." (XVIII: 59) Act we must, but we have the choice to do it selfishly or selflessly. Work done selflessly, for the good of others around us, with the idea, "I am but a servant of God, it is His command that I carry out," leads to a transformation within us. We shall discover in ourselves a greater peace, a clearer conscience, less pressure of likes and dislikes, and more freedom from the clutches of desire and anger. This inner change is what makes us competent to truly enjoy the benefits of the study of Vedanta. "Worshipping Him (God) through one's own work, a man attains perfection", says Lord Krishna (XVIII: 46). By the word "perfection" he means fitness for the discipline of Knowledge.

Moving around everywhere and buzzing noisily, the bees search for flowers. As they find a flower and taste the honey they become quiet. This can symbolize *pravṛtti* and *nivṛtti*. Note that if a bee simply stays put somewhere without finding a flower, it would be far from peaceful. So is the case with man; he must live a life of noble motives and meritorious actions (the movement in search of a flower); then he gains an inner unfoldment (finding the flower) where he is in a position to taste the (nectar of) Self-knowledge!

Preparing for Knowledge

One tends to commit two errors as far as one's understanding of work is concerned. First, one may think of clinging to work forever. In the past, the *karma-kāṇḍī* represented this type. Secondly, one thinks one can straightaway go for Self-knowledge and attain liberation. Those who hastily join some ashram and take initiation to a renunciate's life, without an adequate inner purification, pay for this error.

The commentaries of Shankara on the sacred texts deal much with the first error. One must not stay stuck with *pravṛtti* through any subtle attachment. However meritorious our work may be, it is inherently based on the "I am the doer" idea. Liberation ensues when the Self, which is ever free, is released from all notions of doership. One cannot consider oneself as a doer and as a non-doer at the same time. Thus, when one has purified oneself through selfless action, one must devote oneself to the discipline of knowledge, which belongs to *nivṛtti dharma*. A seeker must understand that the notion, "I work for the good of the society" is also a subtle expression of ego! When one has gained true Knowledge, the question of whether one must or must not work does not arise. A man of wisdom serves the world in either way, we know that his silence and his actions both have immense value to the world.

When we act egoistically, from our personal desires, our pride and prejudice necessarily corrupt the work. In physics, when a conducting wire has a lot of resistance, the electrical power being conveyed through it suffers "losses" all along the wire. What reaches the user-end is less than what was sent from the source. In the same way, our ego (resistance) prevents the all-blissful God-Consciousness in us from beaming out in its entire splendor. A person of wisdom may be compared to a "super-conductor" with zero resistance (no ego) through whom divinity shines in all its glory. Thus *karma yoga* leading to *jñāna* taken up by a spiritual seeker is like the super-conductor research of the physicists, which can bring wonderful rewards to us.

From the context of spirituality and a soul's liberation, any work done with the intent of personal gain, or to satisfy one's own gross or subtle cravings, is ego-prompted activity (*sakāma karma*). This chains one to the world and worldliness by fortifying the ego, and strengthening the foundation of ignorance in one. It is not the quantity, nor any specific area of work that makes our action merit the description as "service." When work is offered lovingly to the Lord, purely with the intention that the work will benefit someone in need, it becomes service. This serves to thin the ego, purify our inner equipment of mind and intellect and prepare us for receiving the right knowledge of the Self. But really the service finds its consummation in the *jñānī* only when he has shed even the thought that he is helping anyone.

VI

Steps to Realization

by Swami Vivekananda

First among the qualifications required of the aspirant for *jñāna*, or wisdom comes *śama* and *dama*, which may be taken together.They mean the keeping of the organs in their own centers without allowing them to stray out. I shall explain to you first what the word *organ* means. Here are the eyes. The eyes are not the organs of vision, but only the instruments. Unless the organs also are present, I cannot see, even if I have eyes. But given both the organs and the instruments, unless the mind attaches itself to these two, no vision takes place. So in each act of perception, three things are necessary: first the external instruments, then the internal organs, and lastly the mind. If any one of them were absent, then there will be no perception. Thus the mind acts through two agencies — one external and the other internal. When I see things, my mind goes out, becomes externalized. But suppose I close my eyes and begin to think. The mind does not go out; it is internally active. But in either case there is activity of the organs. So in order to control the mind, we must first be able to control these organs. To restrain the mind from wandering outward or inward, and to keep the organs in their respective centers, is what is meant by the words *śama* and *dama*. *Śama* consists in not allowing the mind to externalize, and *dama*, in checking the external instruments.

Now comes *uparati*, which consists in not thinking of the things of the senses. Most of our time is spent in thinking about sense objects, things which we have seen or we have heard, which we shall see or shall hear, things which we have eaten or are eating or shall eat, places where we have lived, and so on. We think of them or talk of them most of the time. One who wishes to be a Vedantist must give up this habit.

Then comes the next preparation, (It is a hard task to be a philosopher!) *titikṣā*, the most difficult of all. It is nothing less than the ideal forbearance — "Resist not evil." This requires a little explanation. We may not resist an evil, but at the same time we feel miserable. A person may say very harsh things to me, and I may not outwardly hate him for it, may not answer him back, and may restrain myself from apparently getting angry, but anger and hatred may be in my mind, and I may feel very badly toward that person. That is not nonresistance. I should be without any feeling of hatred or anger, without any thought of resistance. My mind must then be as calm as if nothing had happened. And only when I have got to that state have I attained nonresistance, and not before. Forbearance of all misery, without even a thought of resisting or driving it out, without even any painful feeling in the mind or any remorse — this is *titikṣā*.

The next qualification required is *śraddhā*, faith. One must have tremendous faith in religion and God. Until one has it, one cannot aspire to be a *jñānī*. A great sage once told me that not one in twenty million in this world believed in God. I asked him why, and he told me: "Suppose there is a thief in this room, and he comes to know that there is a mass of gold in the next room with only a very thin partition between the two rooms. What will be the condition of that thief?" I answered: "He will not be able to sleep at all. His brain will be actively thinking of some means of getting at the gold, and he will think of nothing else." Then he replied: "Do you believe that a man could believe in God and not go mad to get Him? If a man sincerely believes that there is that immense, infinite mine of bliss, and that it can be reached, would not that man go mad in his struggle to reach it?" Strong faith in God and the consequent eagerness to reach Him constitute *śraddhā*.

Then comes *samādhāna*, or constant practice, to hold the mind in God. Nothing is done in a day. Religion cannot be swallowed in the form of a pill. It requires hard and constant practice. The mind can be conquered only by slow and steady practice.

The Desire to be Free

Next is *mumukṣuttva*, the intense desire to be free. All the misery we have is of our own choosing — such is our nature. A person who, having been kept in prison for sixty years, was released on the coronation of a new emperor, exclaimed when he came out that he could not live. He must go back to his horrible dungeon among the rats and mice. He could not bear the light. So he asked them to kill him or send him back to the prison, and he was sent back. Similar is the condition of all men. We run headlong after all sorts of misery and are unwilling to be freed from them. Every day we run after pleasure, and before we reach it, we find it is gone. It has slipped through our fingers. Still we do not cease from our mad pursuit, but on and on we go, blinded fools that we are.

Few men know that with pleasure there is pain, and with pain, pleasure; and as pain is disgusting, so is pleasure, since it is the twin brother of pain. It is derogatory to the glory of man that he should be going after pain, and equally derogatory that he should be going after pleasure. Both should be turned aside by men whose reason is balanced. Why will not men seek freedom from being played upon? This moment we are whipped, and when we begin to weep, nature gives us a dollar. Again we are whipped, and when we weep, nature gives us a piece of gingerbread and we begin to laugh again. The sage wants liberty. He finds that sense objects are all vain and that there is no end to pleasures and pains.

How the rich people in the world want to find fresh pleasures! All pleasures are old, and they want new ones. Do you not see how many foolish things they are inventing every day just to titillate the nerves for a moment, and that done, how there comes a reaction? The majority of people are just like a flock of sheep. If the leading sheep falls into a ditch, all the rest follow and break their necks. In the same way, what one leading member of a society does all the others do, without thinking what they are doing.

When a man begins to see the vanity of worldly things, he will feel he ought not to be thus played upon or borne along by nature. That is slavery. If a man has a few kind words said to him, he begins to smile, and when he hears a few harsh words, he begins to weep. He is a slave to a bit of bread, to a breath of air — a slave to dress, a slave to patriotism, to country, to name and fame. He is thus in the midst of slavery, and the real man has become buried within through his bondage. What you call a man is really a slave. When one realizes all this slavery, then comes the intense desire to be free. If a piece of burning charcoal is placed on a man's head, see how he struggles to throw it off. Similar will be the struggles for freedom of a man who really understands that he is a slave of nature.

The next discipline is also a very difficult one: *nityānitya viveka* — discriminating between that which is true and that, which is untrue, between the eternal and the transitory. God alone is eternal; everything else is transitory. Everything dies. The angels die, men die, animals die, earths die, sun, moon, and stars all die; everything undergoes constant change. The mountains of today were the oceans of yesterday and will be oceans tomorrow. Everything is in a state of flux. The whole universe is a mass of change. But there is One who never changes, and that is God. And the nearer we get to Him, the less will be the change for us, the less will nature be able to work on us, and when we reach Him and stand with Him, we shall conquer nature. We shall be masters of these phenomena of nature, and they will have no effect on us.

Why is this discipline so necessary? Because religion is not attained through the ears, nor through the eyes, nor yet through the brain. No scriptures can make us religious. We may study all the books that are in the world, yet we may not understand a word of religion or of God. We may talk all our lives and yet may not be the better for it. We may be the most intellectual people the world ever saw, and yet we may not come to God at all. ...

Cultivating a Pure Heart

It is not at all necessary to be educated or learned to get to God. A sage once told me, "To kill others one must be equipped with swords and shields, but to commit suicide a needle is sufficient; so to teach others, much intellect and learning are necessary, but not so for your own self-illumination." Are you pure? If you are pure, you will reach God. Jesus said, "Blessed are the pure in heart, for they shall see God." If you are not pure, and you know all the sciences in the world, that will not help at all. You may be buried in all the books you read, but that will not be of much use. It is the heart that reaches the goal. Follow the heart. A pure heart sees beyond the intellect; it gets inspired; it knows things that reason can never know, and whenever there is conflict between the pure heart and the intellect, always side with the pure heart, even if you think what your heart is doing is unreasonable. When it is desirous of doing good to others, your brain may tell you that it is not expedient to do so, but follow your heart, and you will find that you make less mistakes than by following your intellect. The pure heart is the best mirror for the reflection of truth, so all these disciplines are for the purification of the heart. And as soon as it is pure, all truths flash upon it in a minute; all truth in the universe will manifest in your heart if you are sufficiently pure.

The great truths about atoms, the finer elements, and the fine perceptions of men, were discovered ages ago by men who never saw a telescope, a microscope, or a laboratory. How did they know all these things? It was through the heart; they purified the heart. It is up to us to do the same today; it is the cultivation of the heart, really, and not that of the intellect that will lessen the misery of the world.

Intellect has been cultured with the result that hundreds of sciences have been discovered, and their effect has been that the few have made slaves of the many — that is all the good that has been done. Artificial desires have been created; and every poor man, whether he has money or not, wants to have those desires satisfied. Some make such strenuous struggle that sometimes they die in the struggle. This is the result. So the way to solve the problem of misery in the world is not through the intellect, but through the heart. If all this vast amount of effort had been spent in making men purer, gentler, more forbearing, this world would be a much happier place. Always cultivate the heart; through the heart the Lord speaks, and through the intellect you yourself speak.

You remember in the Old Testament where Moses was told, "Take off thy shoes from off thy feet, for the place whereon thou standest is holy ground." We must always approach the study of religion with that reverent attitude. He who comes with a pure heart and a reverent attitude, his heart will be opened; the doors will open for him, and he will see the truth.

If you come with the intellect only, you can have a little intellectual gymnastic, intellectual theory, but not truth. Truth has such a face that any one who sees it becomes convinced. The sun does not require a light to show it; the sun is self-effulgent. If truth requires evidence, what will evidence that evidence? If something is necessary as witness for truth, where is the witness for that witness? We must approach religion with reverence and with love, and our heart will stand up and say; this is truth, and this is untruth.

Direct Perception

The field of religion is beyond our senses, beyond even our consciousness. We cannot *sense* God. Nobody has seen God with his eyes or ever will see; nobody has God in his consciousness. I am not conscious of God, or you, or anybody. Where is God? Where is the field of religion? It is beyond the senses, beyond consciousness. Consciousness is only one of the many planes in which we work. You will have to transcend the field of consciousness, go beyond the senses, approach nearer and nearer to your own center, and as you do that, you will approach nearer and nearer to God. What is the proof of God? Direct perception, *pratyakṣa*. The proof of this wall is that I perceive it. God has been perceived that way by thousands before, and will be perceived by all who want to perceive Him. But this perception is not sense perception at all. It is supersensuous, superconscious, and all this training is needed to take us beyond the senses.

By means of all sorts of past work and attachments we are being dragged downward. These preparations will make us pure and light. Bondage will fall off by itself, and we shall be buoyed up beyond this plane of sense perception to which we are tied down. Then we shall see and hear and feel things, which men in the three ordinary states — waking, dream, and sleep — neither feel nor see nor hear. Then we shall speak a strange language, as it were, and the world will not understand us, because it does not know anything but the senses.

True religion is entirely transcendental. Every being that is in the universe has the potentiality of transcending the senses. Even the little worm will one day transcend the senses and reach God. No life will be a failure; there is no such thing as failure in the universe. A hundred times man will hurt himself, a thousand times he will tumble, but in the end he will realize that he is God. We know there is no progress in a straight line. Every soul moves, as it were, in a circle and will have to complete it, and no soul can go so low but there will come a time when it will have to go upward. No one will be lost. We are all projected from one common center, which is God. The highest as well as the lowest life God ever projected will come back to the Father of all lives. "From whom all beings are projected, in whom all live, and unto whom they all return — that is God."

VII

Four Steps to Wisdom

by Anthony de Mello

To acquire happiness you don't have to do anything, because happiness cannot be acquired. Does anybody know why? Because we have it already. How can you acquire what you already have? Then why don't you experience it? Because you've got to drop something. Life is easy; life is delightful. It is only hard on your illusions, your ambitions, your greed, and your cravings. Do you know where these things come from? From having identified with all kinds of labels.

The first thing you need to do is get in touch with negative feelings that you are not even aware of. Lots of people have negative feelings they're not aware of. Lots of people are depressed and they're not aware they are depressed. It's only when they make contact with joy that they understand how depressed they were. You can't deal with a cancer that you haven't detected. You can't get rid of boll weevils on your farm if you're not aware of their existence. The first thing you need is awareness of your negative feelings. What negative feelings? Gloominess, for instance. You're feeling gloomy and moody. You feel self-hatred or guilt. You feel that life is pointless, and it makes no sense; you've got hurt feelings, you're feeling nervous and tense. Get in touch with those feelings first.

The second step (this is a four-step program) is to understand that the feeling is in you, not in reality. That's such a self-evident thing, but do you think people know it? They don't, believe me. They've got Ph.D.s and are presidents of universities, but they haven't understood this. They didn't teach me how to live at school. They taught me everything else. As one man said, "I got a pretty good education. It took me years to get over it." That's what spirituality is all about, you know: unlearning. Unlearning all the rubbish they taught you.

Negative feelings are in you, not in reality. So stop trying to change reality. That's crazy! Stop trying to change the other person. We spend all our time and energy trying to change external circumstances, trying to change our spouses, our bosses, our friends, our enemies, and everybody else. We don't have to change anything. Negative feelings are in *you*. No person on earth has the power to make you unhappy. There is no event on earth that has the power to disturb you or hurt you. No event, condition, situation, or person. Nobody told you this; they told you the opposite. That's why you're in the mess that you're in right now. That is why you're asleep. They never told you this. But it's self-evident.

Let's suppose that rain washes out a picnic. Who is feeling negative? The rain? Or you? What's causing the negative feeling? The rain or your reaction? When you bump your knee against a table, the table's fine. It's busy being what it was made to be — a table. The pain is in your knee, not in the table. The mystics keep trying to tell us that reality is all right. Reality is not problematic. Problems exist only in the human mind. We might add, in the stupid, sleeping human mind. Reality is not problematic. Take away human beings from this planet and life would go on, nature would go on in all its loveliness and violence. Where would the problem be? No problem. You created the problem. You are the problem. You identified with "me" and that is the problem. The feeling is in you, not in reality.

Be Free

The third step: Never identify with that feeling. It has nothing to do with the *I*. Don't define your essential self in terms of that feeling. Don't say, "I am depressed." If you want to say, "It is depressed," that's all right. If you want to say depression is there, that's fine; if you want to say gloominess is there, that's fine. But not: I am gloomy. You're defining yourself in terms of the feeling. That's your illusion; that's your mistake. There is a depression there right now, there are hurt feelings there right now, but let it be, leave it alone. It will pass. Everything passes, everything. Your depressions and your thrills have nothing to do with happiness. Those are the swings of the pendulum. If you seek kicks or thrills, get ready for depression. Do you want your drug? Get ready for the hangover. One end of the pendulum swings to the other.

This has nothing to do with *I*; it has nothing to do with happiness. It is the *me*. If you remember this, if you say it to yourself a thousand times, if you try these three steps a thousand times, you will get it. You might not need to do it even three times. I don't know; there's no rule for it. But do it a thousand times and you'll make the biggest discovery in your life. To hell with those gold mines in Alaska. What are you going to do with that gold? If you're not happy, you can't live. So you found gold. What does that matter? You're a king; you're a princess. You're free; you don't care anymore about being accepted or rejected, that makes no difference. Psychologists tell us how important it is to get a sense of belonging. Baloney! Why do you want to belong to anybody? It doesn't matter anymore.

A friend of mine told me that there's an African tribe where capital punishment consists of being ostracized. If you were kicked out of New York, or wherever you're residing, you wouldn't die. How is it that the African tribesman died? He dies because he partakes of the common stupidity of humanity. He thinks he will not be able to live if he does not belong. It's very different from most people, or is it? He's convinced he needs to belong. But you don't need to belong to anybody or anything or any group. You don't even need to be in love. Who told you you do? What you need is to be free. What you need is to love. That's it; that's your nature. But what you're really telling me is that you want to be desired. You want to be applauded, to be attractive, to have all the little monkeys running after you.

You're wasting your life. *Wake up!* You don't need this. You can be blissfully happy without it.

Your society is not going to be happy to hear this, because you become terrifying when you open your eyes and understand this. How do you control a person like this? He doesn't need you; he's not threatened by your criticism; he doesn't care what you think of him or what you say about him. He's cut all those strings; he's not a puppet any longer. It's terrifying. "So we've got to get rid of him. He tells the truth; he has become fearless; he has stopped being human." *Human!* Behold! A human being at last! He broke out of his slavery, broke out of their prison.

No event justifies a negative feeling. There is no situation in the world that justifies a negative feeling. That's what all our mystics have been crying themselves hoarse to tell us. But nobody listens. The negative feeling is in you. In the *Bhagavad Gītā*, the sacred book of the Hindus, Lord Krishna says to Arjuna, "Plunge into the heat of battle and keep your heart at the lotus feet of the Lord." A marvelous sentence.

You don't have to do anything to acquire happiness. The great Meister Eckhart said very beautifully, "God is not attained by a process of addition to anything in the soul, but by a process of subtraction." You don't do anything to be free, you drop something. Then you're free.

It reminds me of the Irish prisoner who dug a tunnel under the prison wall and managed to escape. He comes out right in the middle of a school playground where little children are playing. Of course, when he emerges from the tunnel he can't restrain himself anymore and begins to jump up and down, crying, "I'm free, I'm free, I'm free!" A little girl there looks at him scornfully and says, "That's nothing. I'm four."

The fourth step: How do you change things? How do you change yourselves? There are many things you must understand here, or rather, just one thing that can be expressed in many ways. Imagine a patient who goes to a doctor and tells him what he is suffering from. The doctor says, "Very well, I've understood your symptoms. Do you know what I will do? I will prescribe a medicine for your neighbor!" The patient replies, "Thank you very much, Doctor, that makes me feel much better." Isn't that absurd? But that's what we all do. The person who is asleep always thinks he'll feel better if somebody else changes. You're suffering because you are asleep, but you're thinking, "How wonderful life would be if somebody else would change; how wonderful life would be if my neighbor changed, my wife changed, my boss changed."

We always want someone else to change so that we will feel good. But has it ever struck you that even if your wife changes or your husband changes, what does that do to you? You're just as vulnerable as before; you are just as idiotic as before; you're just as asleep as before. You are the one who needs to change, who needs to take medicine. You keep insisting, "I feel good because the world is right." *Wrong*! The world is right because I feel good. That's what all the mystics are saying.

VIII

Unlearning

by Hazrat Inayat Khan

It is most difficult to forget what one has once learned. Learning is one thing, and unlearning is another. The process of spiritual attainment is through unlearning. People consider their belief to be their religion. In reality, belief is a steppingstone to religion. Besides, if I were to picture belief, it is just like a staircase that leads on to higher realization. But instead of going up the staircase people stand on it. It is just like running water that does not flow any more. People have made their belief rigid, and therefore instead of being benefited by their belief they are going backwards. If it were not so, one would have thought that all the believers in God, in truth, and the hereafter would be better than the unbelievers are. But what happens is that they are worse, because they have nailed their own feet to their belief.

Very often I am in a position where I can say very little, especially when a person comes to me with his preconceived ideas and wants to take my direction, my guidance on the spiritual path; yet at the same time his first intention is to see if his thoughts fit in with mine and if my thoughts fit in with his thoughts. He cannot make himself empty for the direction given. He has not come to follow my thoughts, but wants to confirm to himself that his idea is right. Among a hundred persons who come for spiritual guidance, ninety come out of that tap. What does it show? That they do not want to give up their own idea, but they want to have it confirmed that the idea they have is right.

Spiritual attainment, from beginning to end, is unlearning what one has learned. But how does one unlearn? What one has learned is in oneself. One can do it by becoming wiser. The wiser one becomes, the more one is able to contradict one's own ideas. The less wisdom one has, the more one holds to one's own ideas. In the wisest person there is willingness to submit to others. And the most foolish person is always ready to stand firm to support his own ideas. The reason is that the wise person can easily give up his thought; the foolish holds on to it. That is why he does not become wise — because he sticks to his own ideas; that is why he does not progress.

Mental Purification

Mental purification therefore is the only method by which one can reach the spiritual goal. In order to accomplish this, one has to look at another person's point of view. For in reality every point of view is one's own point of view. The vaster one becomes, the greater the realization that comes to one, the more one sees that every point of view is all right. If one is able to expand oneself to the consciousness of another person, one's consciousness becomes as large as two persons. And so it can be as large as a thousand persons when one accustoms oneself to try and see what others think.

The next step in mental purification is to be able to see the right of the wrong and the wrong of the right, and the evil of the good and the good of the evil. It is a difficult task, but once one has accomplished this, one rises above good and evil.

One must be able to see the pain in pleasure and the pleasure in pain; the gain in the loss and the loss in the gain. What generally happens is that one is blunted to one thing and that one's eyes are open to another thing; that one does not see the loss or that one does not see the gain; if one recognizes the right, one does not recognize the wrong.

Mental purification means that impressions such as good and bad, wrong and right, gain and loss, and pleasure and pain, these opposites which block the mind, must be cleared out by seeing the opposite of these things. Then one can see the enemy in the friend and the friend in the enemy. When one can recognize poison in nectar and nectar in the poison, that is the time when death and life become one too. Opposites no more remain opposites before one. That is called mental purification. And those who come to this stage are the living sages.

The third field of mental purification is to identify oneself with what one is not. By this one purifies one's mind from impressions of one's own false identity.

The Story of a Sage

I will give as an example the story of a sage in India. The story begins by saying that a young man in his youth asked his mother, who was a peasant woman living in a village, "What is the best occupation, mother?" And the mother said, "I do not know, son, except that those who searched after the highest in life went in search of God." "Then where must I go, mother?" he asked. She answered, "I do not know whether it is practical or not, but they say in the solitude, in the forest." So he went there for a long time and lived a life of patience and solitude. And once or twice in between he came to see his mother. Sometimes his patience was exhausted, his heart broken. Sometimes he was disappointed in not finding God. And each time the mother sent him back with stronger advice. At the third visit he said, "Now I have been there a long time." "Yes," said his mother, "now I think you are ready to go to a teacher." So he went to see a teacher. And there were many pupils learning under that teacher. Every pupil had a little room to himself for meditation, and this pupil also was told to go into a certain room to meditate. The teacher asked, "Is there anything you love in the world?" This young man, having been away from home since childhood, having not seen anything of the world, could think of no one that he knew, except for the little cow that was in his house. He said, "I love the cow in our house." The teacher said, "Then think of the cow in your meditation."

All the other pupils came and went, and sat in their room for fifteen minutes for a little meditation; then they got tired and went away; but this young man remained sitting there from the time the teacher had told him. After some time the teacher asked, "Where is he?" The other pupils answered, "We don't know. He must be in his room." They went to look for him; the door was closed and there was no answer. The teacher went himself and opened the door, and there he saw the pupil sitting in meditation, fully absorbed in it. And when the teacher called him by name, he answered with the sound of a cow. The teacher said, "Come out." He answered, "My horns are too large to pass through the door." Then the teacher said to his pupils, "Look, this is the living example of meditation. You are meditating on God and you do not know where God is, but he is meditating on the cow and he has become the cow; he has lost his identity. He has identified himself with the object on which he meditates."

Stilling the Mind

All the difficulty of our life is that we cannot come out of a false conception. Therefore the third aspect of mental purification is to be able to identify oneself with something else. The Sufis have their own way of teaching it. Very often one holds the idea of one's spiritual teacher; and with that idea one gains the knowledge and inspiration and power that the spiritual teacher has. It is just like a heritage.

The man who cannot concentrate so much as to forget himself and go deep into the subject, on whom he concentrates, will not succeed in mastering concentration. The fourth mental purification is to free oneself from a form and have the sense of the abstract. Everything suggests to the eye a form, everything;

even so much that if the name of a person whom one has never seen is mentioned, one makes a form of him. Even such things as fairies and spirits and angels, as soon as they are mentioned, are always pictured in a certain form. This is a hindrance to attaining the presence of the formless; and therefore this mental purification is of very great importance. Its purpose is to be able to think of an idea without form. No doubt this is only attained by great concentration and meditation, but once it is attained it is most satisfactory.

And the fifth way is to be able to repose one's mind. In other words, to relax the mind. Imagine, after having toiled for the whole day, how much the body stands in need of rest; how much more then must the mind stand in need of rest!

The mind works much faster than the body; naturally the mind is much more tired than the body. And not every person knows how to rest his mind, and therefore the mind never has a rest. And then what happens after a while is that the mind becomes feeble; it loses memory, the power of action; it loses reason. The worst effects are mostly brought about by not giving the mind proper repose. If such infirmities as doubt and fear happen to enter the mind, then a person becomes restless. He can never find rest, for at night the mind continues on the track of the same impressions. Simple as it seems to be, very few know the resting of the mind and how wonderful it is in itself. And what power, what inspiration, comes as a reaction from it, and what peace does one experience by it, and how it helps the body and mind! The spirit is renewed once the mind has had its rest.

The first step towards the resting of the mind is the relaxation of the body. If one is able to relax one's muscular and nervous system at will, then the mind is automatically refreshed. Besides that, one must be able to cast away anxiety, worries, doubts, and fears by the power of will, putting oneself in a restful state; this will be accomplished by the help of proper breathing.

Great magnetism is produced by having stilled and purified the mind. And the lack of it causes lack of magnetism. The presence of those whose mind is not purified and stilled becomes a source of unrest for others as well as for themselves. And they attract little because the power of attraction is lost; everyone is tired by their presence, and their atmosphere causes uneasiness and discomfort. They are a burden to themselves and others.

Once the mind is purified, the next step is the cultivation of the heart quality, which culminates in spiritual attainment.

IX

Meditation and God-Realization

by *Swami Satprakashananda*

[The following article is transcribed and edited by Ray Ellis from a lecture given by Swami Satprakashananda.]

There is only one way to God-realization — and that is medita-tion. There are many subsidiary means to God-realization, but the primary means, the direct means, is meditation. Other spiri-tual disciplines prepare the mind and the body for the practice of meditation, but until the mind is completely absorbed in medita-tion on God, He is not revealed to the individual consciousness.

By God-realization is meant the direct perception of God. You can know about God by hearing about Him, by reasoning about Him, and by thinking about Him. All scriptural study, lis-tening to sermons or philosophical speculation gives indirect knowledge of God. Most seekers of God have this indirect knowledge to some extent at least, but what does the seeker need for the direct perception of God? Just as this daylight is clearly manifest to a person, similarly that Supreme Reality must be manifest to him. It is the direct perception of Reality that re-moves forever all bondage, suffering and limitation. In spite of our indirect knowledge of God, we are subject to many weak-nesses. What is needed is to convert this indirect knowledge into direct experience. And for that, meditation is absolutely necessary. You may pray to God, you may sing devotional songs, but until your mind becomes completely absorbed in God, God will not be manifest to you. In order to realize God, you have to practice meditation.

God-realization cannot be achieved in a day or two. You have to practice continually, day after day. But before you can adopt the practice of meditation, you have to develop loving devotion to God. Unless your mind longs for the realization of God, you cannot take up the practice of meditation with any success. You have to go through certain preliminary courses in order to rid the mind of the attachment to the temporal and also to develop true longing for God, true devotion to God. This is why in all religious courses moral principles have been included to discipline the body and the mind. You should perform the duties of life, associate with spiritually minded persons, and go through certain religious courses, worshipping God in different ways. If a person has the least inkling of spirituality, the least yearning for God-realization, he should adopt these methods and try to develop that yearning into loving devotion to God. These are the practical courses. What is needed is the urge to follow these courses.

As far as possible you must practice righteousness. You have to perform your duties faithfully and efficiently as far as your situation in life and capacities permit. You must avoid adverse influences in life as much as possible. What is the good of losing time gossiping and mixing with all sorts of people and seeing all kinds of scenery? A congenial atmosphere and associating with holy people is very much needed. Just as they are needed for your physical development, so they are needed for your mental development, and they are needed for your spiritual development too.

Then you should follow some religious courses. Try to worship the Lord in different ways. There are physical methods, verbal methods, and mental methods. Adopt one or two of these methods and practice them with faith, patience, and perseverance. You will then surely increase your devotion to God. Until you develop a measure of inner purity, at least some freedom from attachment to the sense objects, and some devotion to God, you cannot practice meditation successfully. These courses you should go through, and even when starting meditation, you should continue these practices.

The Right Knowledge of God

A person who wants the direct experience of God should have the right conception or knowledge of God. Otherwise, one will be misled in the world of imagination. God cannot be realized through imagination. No doubt, in meditation there is some play of imagination, but that imagination is based on the understanding of God's nature, on the right knowledge of God's nature. This is necessary, as without it, one may get trapped in a world of fantasy. One should know that God is above all, self-luminous, pure awareness, Consciousness Itself.

Just as this psychophysical system is ruled over by a central principle of consciousness, similarly the whole universe is ruled over by a principle of consciousness immanent in the universe. That is God. He is not apart from anything. He is the reality underlying everything. He is the self-shining Consciousness. We live in Him, we move in Him and we have our being in Him, because He is the very soul of the universe. What sustains the psychophysical system? One luminous principle. Similarly, the whole universe is also sustained by one luminous, supreme principle. And that supreme principle is the indwelling Self in each and every one of us. This is why the way to God is an inner approach. You may explore the whole world, the entire space, but you cannot find God, because you will always be moving in the sense world, in the phenomenal world.

The eyes cannot perceive Him. He is not an object having a color or a form. The ears cannot hear Him. None of the senses can perceive Him. He is beyond all sense perception. The hands cannot grasp Him. This physical body cannot reach Him. He is beyond the perception of the sense organs. He is also beyond the reach of the organs of action as well as of human thought. How can we reach Him? He can be contacted only by this individual consciousness. Pure spirit can be contacted only through spirit. So Vedanta, which emphasizes the direct perception of God, always stresses this point: that God is the innermost Self of all, and the way to God is an inner way. Yoga, which means the unification of the individual self with the Supreme Self, is necessary. And that is done through meditation.

Turning the Mind Inward

You cannot reach God simply by looking outside and moving here and there. You have to dive deep within yourself. That is why the mind should be turned inward. Instead of turning the mind outward, you have to turn its rays inward. That Supreme Spirit is very hard to grasp with the mind. So you have to adopt some concrete form in order to concentrate the mind on the Supreme Spirit. You may adopt the form of a great spiritual leader. These great spiritual leaders are simply the embodiments of God-consciousness. They are the best manifestations of God the world has ever seen, the best manifestations of divine power, divine wisdom, divine love, divine freedom, divine purity, and divine joy. But if these personal forms do not appeal to an individual, he or she can take some other, impersonal form — anything that represents divine purity, divine consciousness. A flower can be a symbol, a flame of light can be a symbol, and the sun can be a symbol of divinity. Concentrate the mind on that, knowing that this luminous object is the symbol of Supreme Consciousness, and this particular form one meditates on is simply the embodiment of God-consciousness. If a person concentrates the mind on that form, knowing the meaning of the form, then gradually the mind becomes absorbed, and the reality underlying that form, the reality symbolized by that form, becomes revealed.

What is done in meditation is this: The ego-consciousness of the individual soul is unified with the Supreme Self, or Supreme Consciousness. This is done through the mind. As one concentrates the mind on God, the ego — which is a function of the mind, and through which consciousness shines as the individual soul — becomes joined with the Reality. The barrier is gradually eliminated. Eventually, this seemingly limited consciousness becomes joined, unified, with the Supreme Consciousness. When this 'I', the knower, the perceiver, the experiencer, the worshiper, the meditator, becomes joined with the object of meditation, with the object of worship, then these two form one reality. They coalesce. If a wife thinks of the husband very lovingly, devotedly, with full concentration of the mind, she is likely to forget herself and in her consciousness only her husband will abide. Similarly, through deep meditation, the distinction between the meditator and the object is bridged and one Reality shines. Supreme Consciousness alone becomes manifest. This individualized consciousness enters into universal Consciousness and becomes part and parcel of That. This is the state of *samādhī*, the fruition of meditation.

The Non-Dualistic Experience

What is the tripartite division in all knowledge? The knower, the known, and the process of knowledge. These three exist in every knowledge. Whether it is direct knowledge or indirect knowledge, there are these three factors. When one meditates, this distinction is eliminated. The knower becomes united with the known, and the process of knowledge also does not exist. At the highest reach of this state, the I-consciousness becomes completely merged in the Supreme Consciousness. Then only one undivided, absolute Consciousness shines. Consciousness cannot be unconscious. Consciousness is quite real to itself. Consciousness shines, who knows it? It knows itself. This individual consciousness is real to itself. No one else comes and tells a person that *is* Consciousness, a self-shining, self-evident reality. It is its own authority. For the existence of an object, an authority is needed — "I see it, so it is" — but this Consciousness, ever shining, is its own authority. On the authority of this, every other form of existence is based. Even God's existence is based on the authority of this! Who establishes the reality of God? Who says God exists? Some individual says God exists. He experiences God, or thinks that God exists, or he believes that God exists. So that Supreme Consciousness beyond all distinctions of knower and known, is its own authority, self-evident. If this individual consciousness, in spite of all seeming limitations, is self-evident and is its own authority, and can stand the challenge of everyone else, why cannot that Supreme Consciousness be its own authority? At that stage when this individual consciousness becomes merged completely in that Supreme Consciousness, one integral, undivided, limitless, pure Consciousness shines. That is the non-dualistic experience, called *nirvikalpa samādhī.*

Somehow or the other, in certain cases, this individuality is retained and comes back to what we call the normal state. But when such a person comes back, that experience still continues, and he sees Consciousness as the one Reality, penetrating everything and everyone. He sees that everything is suffused with that Light. His own ego-consciousness is also suffused with the Supreme Consciousness. Though he apparently lives in the body, he knows himself as one with the Supreme Consciousness. Such persons are considered *jīvanmukta,* that is, they are free even while living in the body.

The Dualistic Experience

But all spiritual aspirants do not reach that, nor do they aspire to reach it. They realize God in what is called the personal aspect. That realization also comes in the same way — through meditation. The mind is concentrated on God with attributes, God as the beloved. He is the Supreme Reality, and that Supreme Reality is meditated on as the Supreme object of love. Just as through love this individual consciousness is completely lost in the consciousness of the beloved, similarly in the meditation on God, this individual consciousness becomes unified with God-consciousness. The individuality is not lost and completely merged, but one realizes oneself as belonging wholly to that Supreme Reality, as a part and parcel of It. There is unity but with a distinction. That is to say it falls short of complete identification. When one comes back to this consciousness of the physical body, then also one knows that one Supreme Self sustains this universe, and that Supreme Self is also the indwelling spirit in each and every individual. That state of *samādhi* in which this individual consciousness is retained, and in which the individual knows himself as belonging to the Supreme Reality, is called *savikalpa samādhi*.

These are the two ways (*nirvikalpa* and *savikalpa samādhī*) by which God can be directly perceived or realized. One can meditate on God through different forms. It is said that for many saints God appeared in the very form on which He was meditated. Some saints have seen God in the form of Jesus Christ, and some have seen God in the form of Krishna. Shri Ramakrishna saw God in many different forms. However, seeing God in a particular form is not the culmination of spiritual realization. If a person sees God in a particular form, it need not be a hallucination because God often does assume form and appear before a devotee. But this realization does not free a devotee completely. He reaches a high stage of development, he becomes free from many weaknesses, he becomes established to a great extent in freedom, in wisdom and in joy, but still he cannot perceive God constantly. By direct perception of God, or God-realization in the true sense, is meant perceiving God as the Supreme Consciousness immanent in the universe. That experience can come through meditation. That culminates in *savikalpa* or *nirvikalpa samādhī*.

Preparing for Meditation

You must know the essential need for the practice of meditation for the direct perception of God. If you intensely long to be free from all weaknesses, from the never-ending cycle of birth and death, and from the bondage of karma, and want to be established in eternal freedom, then you have to realize God directly. The *Muṇḍaka Upaniṣad* (II:2.8) says: "When He who is transcendent and immanent is directly perceived, then all doubts leave the mind. All knots are broken. The deposit of karma is removed." You must be convinced of the truth that without God-realization there is no other way out of birth and death, out of this duality of light and darkness, knowledge and ignorance, pain and pleasure. You must be firmly convinced of this. And then you should also know that through meditation alone could you reach this Consciousness.

You have to follow all the preliminary courses preparatory to the practice of meditation. In the *Bhagavad Gītā* the necessity of leading a disciplined life has been very much emphasized, because spiritual practice must be regular and persistent. On this point both Patanjali's Yoga and Vedanta agree. Practice is the secret. It is in fact the secret of proficiency in every field. Simply by 'knowing' the method you cannot gain proficiency. You have to practice it from day to day persistently. At the same time, the mind has to be purified by following the observance of moral principles, association with the right kind of people, the performance of duties, and the practice of prayer and worship. You should be moderate in eating, drinking, talking, sleeping, working, and resting. Unless you live a very moderate life, you cannot make the mind calm. ...

You may not be able to realize God within a short time, or even within a long time, but do not think you are not making any progress. With practice there will be progress — and the pace of progress will be directly proportional to the efforts you put in. In practicing meditation gain is assured. Whether you follow the path of the impersonal, absolute Being, or you follow the path of the personal God, you have got to practice meditation.

According to non-dualistic Vedanta, you should first of all hear about God and have a clear understanding of what God means. You should not rely simply on imagination born of ignorance. The correct meditation in which there is the play of imagination is based on the direct evidence of the seers and saints. First, it is necessary therefore to hear about God. But by hearing you have only the indirect knowledge of God. So, next you have to reason in order to have a clear understanding of what you have heard. Third, when you have a clear understanding through hearing and reflection you must practice meditation. Simply through reasoning you cannot have that perception of Reality. You will be left in the plane of indirect knowledge. Through meditation only you come to realize the impersonal, absolute Being, by converting your indirect knowledge into a direct experience.

In the path of devotion, there are, as I said, physical methods, verbal methods, and mental methods of worship. One may stress the physical methods, but ultimately the mind must be absorbed in the thought of God. There must be the unification of this individual consciousness with the Supreme Consciousness. That is the mark of direct perception. The mind has to be absorbed. God is not an external being whom one can objectify. God is the soul of all souls. He is the innermost Self. He is at the back of this individual consciousness. For this reason the practice of meditation has been very much emphasized. Therefore, some time should be reserved daily for meditation on God. You may say, 'Well, I always think of God.' That is good, but it is not enough for the direct perception of God. Constant remembrance develops love and yearning within a person. But direct perception of God requires something more. You will have to practice meditation. Of course, constant effort to remember God and to think of Him will help the mind to be easily concentrated at the time of meditation. ...

There are practical courses to the attainment of the goal. The goal is very far, very high, but you can reach it. If you start with what is possible for you to practice now, you can gradually move ahead and eventually reach the highest level. The last resort must be meditation. You can practice meditation side by side with all your preliminary practices. No one expects you to have an absolutely pure mind before starting your spiritual practices. You must start straightaway with whatever degree of purity, faith, and longing for God you possess. As devotion increases your capacity to meditate will also increase. You will thus gradually attain the perception of truth.

Japa or the repetition of the mantra or sacred word or formula, is another practice that helps to purify the mind to a great extent. The mantra is symbolic of God-consciousness. Every word has a meaning. Every word is the symbol of an idea. There are some words that are symbols of God-consciousness. There are potent seed-words. These are, as it were, seeds of spiritual consciousness. If you repeat that potent seed-word, it has the capacity to lift your mind to the realm of consciousness of which it is a symbol. Repetition of mantra works in the lower levels of the mind to remove the *saṁskāra* that are deposited at the bottom of the mind until they are gradually eliminated. Without that inner purification, meditation is impossible.

You may safeguard yourself from external disturbances, but that will not be enough for the effective practice of meditation, because the causes of the disturbances are not as much external as internal. The internal disturbances arise from the deposit of past impressions, so these disturbances have to be eliminated or subdued to a great extent. This is achieved through the constant repetition of mantra. Mantras have these twofold capacity: one, they can remove the *saṁskāra* which tie the mind to this gross, sense-level; and two, they have the capacity to lift the thought from the gross, physical level to the realm of pure Spirit. That is why *japa* is very much emphasized in Vedantic literature. It occupies a very important place not only in the Hindu spiritual tradition but also in Islam, Christianity, and Buddhism. So, along with the practice of meditation, *japa* also must be practiced. If both these processes, meditation and *japa*, are adopted, then the highest goal will be gradually reached. Have absolutely no doubt about it.

PART THREE

People of Wisdom

*The inspired sages, free of desires
And full of devotional love
Attain the highest glory and everlasting peace.*

Sāma Veda: 92

From time to time an ancient philosophy needs an intelligent reinterpretation in the context of the new times. Men of wisdom, prophets, and seers must guide the common man as to how he can apply the ancient laws effectively to his present pattern of life.

Swami Chinmayananda

The sages aspiring for a higher and better standard, work with diligence and devotion; they inspire people to do their duty with dedication. This is how nations and communities grow strong.

AtharvaVeda XIX:41.1

X

The Self-Realized Person

by Swami Chinmayananda

The Self-realized person is a dynamic man of action. In order to understand him, however, we must understand him as he lives in the world. How does he see the world? How does he react to problems? How does he relate himself to others? In the *Bhagavad Gītā* (The Divine Song of the Lord) the author, Vyasa, paints a vivid picture of such a man of perfection through the dialogue between Lord Krishna and Arjuna. From the following verse until the end of the chapter, Lord Krishna gives Arjuna a complete and exhaustive description of the inner experience and the outer conduct of a person of steady wisdom. By narrating the inner and outer life of the Self-realized person, Lord Krishna helps us to distinguish the right type of masters from the counterfeit ones. These passages also have a direct appeal to all sincere seekers inasmuch as this section gives them an easy rule of thumb as to what kind of mental attitudes they should develop during their practice, so that they may come to realize the ever-effulgent divinity in themselves, the Pure Awareness.

> When a man completely casts off, O Partha! all the desires of the mind and is satisfied in the Self by the Self, then he is said to be one of steady wisdom. (II:55)

This very opening stanza is a brilliant summary of all that we should know of the mental condition of the perfect one. One is considered a person of wisdom only when one has completely cast away all the desires in one's mind. The intellect is ordinarily enveloped in a mist of ignorance, and when it crosses over the layers of this ignorance, and goes beyond, it comes to rediscover the glory of the Self. Therefore, a person of steady wisdom is one who has reached beyond the veil of ignorance, and as such, not even a trace of ignorance can be found in his intellect. It is the intellect contaminated by ignorance that becomes the breeding-ground for desires. But the one who has gotten rid of his ignorance through right knowledge naturally becomes desireless. By explaining here the absence of the *effects*, the Lord is negating the existence of the *cause*: where desires are not found, ignorance has ended, and true Knowledge comes to shine forth.

If this alone were a deciding factor of the person with steady wisdom, then the Hindu person of wisdom would be condemned as a madman by the modern thinkers, as one who has not the initiative even to desire! Desire at least means the capacity of the mind to project into the future; the ability to think of schemes or patterns in which one can be happier than one is at present. But materialists criticize that the wise man seems to lose even the capacity to do so as he goes beyond his intellect and experiences the Self. But this criticism cannot be applied to this stanza since the second line adds that the perfect one is blissful in his experience of the Self. A perfect man is therefore, defined here, not only as one who no longer has any desire, but also as one who has positively come to enjoy the bliss of the Self.

An infant has his own playmates, and as he grows from childhood to boyhood, he leaves his toys and runs after a new set of things. As the boy grows to be a youth, he again loses his desires for the things of boyhood and craves for yet another set of things. Again, in old age the same entity casts away all objects that were until then providers of great joy to him and comes to demand a totally different set of objects. This is an observed phenomenon. As we grow, our demands also grow. With reference to the new scheme of things demanded, the old ideas are cast away.

The ignorant with their egocentricity have burning desires for the sense objects, binding attachments to emotions, and jealous preferences for their own pet ideas. But when the ego is transcended, when ignorance, like a mist, has lifted itself, and the finite ego stands face to face with the divine Reality, it melts to become one with the Infinite. The person of steady wisdom, who is self-satisfied in the Self, can no more entertain any desire for the paltry objects of the body, mind, or intellect, as he has come to live the very source of all bliss. Vyasa defines such a person here as a man of steady wisdom (*sthitaprajña*), and as it comes from the mouth of Krishna it gathers the divine ring of an incontrovertible Truth.

Equanimity

Having explained that the perfect sage is one who has come to sacrifice all his petty desires in his self-discovered satisfaction in the Self, Krishna here explains that the next characteristic feature by which we can know a sage is by his equanimity in pleasure and pain. If in the last stanza Krishna considered the person as an *actor*, here he is considering him as a *bearer of body-afflictions*.

> He whose mind is not shaken by adversity, who does not hanker after pleasures, who is free from attachment, fear and anger, is called a sage of steady wisdom. (II:56)

One who is stable, whose heart is undisturbed in sorrow or in joy, unattached, fearless, and without anger is described here as a *muni*, a silent sage. Of the emotions that must be absent in one who is a master in all situations, we are told emphatically only of the following three: attachment (*rāga*), fear (*bhaya*) and anger (*krodha*). When the absence of only these three qualities is asserted so emphatically, a sincere student naturally asks: "Is this all? Has Vyasa overlooked all the other possibilities?" But a closer study reveals that in the discussion here he has not committed the crime of inappropriate emphasis upon the non-essentials, as some critics have been tempted to point out. The theme in the earlier stanza was that the perfect person is one who has forsaken all cravings that come up in his mind, and the above stanza asserts the mental stability of such a person. Through the biographies of the perfected ones we can see that almost all of them are an antithesis of an ordinary person. Many emotions that are common to the ordinary person are not at all seen in a perfect one.

In our interactions with the sense objects, we can easily see how our attachments to things and beings create pain and fear. When an individual develops a desire powerful enough to be a strong attachment, he instinctively begins to entertain a sense of fear in case he is not able to secure the object he so deeply desires. And once it has been secured, then again the fear arises for the security of the object acquired. When we have formed a deep attachment to an object and when fear itself begins to disturb us, then our attitude against those that come between ourselves and the object of attachment is called *anger.* Anger is thus nothing but an attachment for an object when expressed towards an obstacle that has come between us and the object of our attachment. The anger thus rising in our mind is directly proportional to the fear we entertain that the obstacle may hold us back from winning the object of our love.

Shankara in his *Vivekacūḍāmaṇi* says that a person of steady wisdom is not distressed by calamities such as (a) those that may arise from the disorders of the body (*ādhyātmika*); (b) those arising from external objects (*ādhibhautika*); and (c) those arising from unseen causes (*ādhidaivika*). Fire increases when fuel is added, but the fire of desire in a perfect one does not increase when more pleasures are attained. Such a one is called a man of steady knowledge, a silent sage.

Without Attachment

In the following verse, Lord Krishna, like an artist inspired by his own theme, is again choosing the right words to add more light and shade to the picture of the perfected one, which he was painting upon the heart of his listener: Arjuna.

> He who is always without attachment, on meeting with anything good or bad who neither rejoices nor hates, his wisdom is fixed. (II:57)

He who without attachment squarely meets life with all equanimity and poise is one who is established in wisdom. Here we also have to understand the entire stanza or else there will be the danger of misinterpreting its true meaning. A mere detachment from the things of life is not a sign of perfection or true discriminative understanding. Many unintelligent enthusiasts actually run away from their duties in life hoping that in the quietude of the jungle they will gain their goal, thinking that they have developed perfect detachment from the sense objects. Arjuna himself had expressed earlier that he would renounce the call of duty and the field of activity, and by thus retiring into quietude the Pandava hero hoped to reach perfection and peace. To dissuade Arjuna from making this calamitous mistake, Krishna started his serious discourse in the second chapter.

Detachment from suicidal affections and unintelligent tenderness in itself cannot take a person to the higher realms of divinity. Detachment from the world outside must be accompanied by a growing inner balance to face all challenges in life, auspicious and inauspicious, in perfect equipoise without any uncontrolled rejoicing at the auspicious, or any aversion for the inauspicious experiences.

A mere detachment in itself is not the way of the perfect life, as it is only a negative existence of constantly escaping from life. To live in *attachment* is living in slavery all throughout our life to the things we are attached to. But the perfect one is one who, with a divine freedom, lives in the world sincerely meeting both the joys and sorrows that life provides for him. In the winter when we lie basking in the rays of the sun we not only enjoy its warmth but at the same time we suffer its glare. To complain of the glare is to bring sorrow into the very enjoyment of the warmth. One who is intelligent will either try to ignore the glare and enjoy the warmth fully, or shade the glare, and bask in the enjoyable warmth.

Similarly, life by its very nature is a mixture of both good and bad, and to live ever adjusting ourselves — avoiding the bad and striving to linger in the experience of the good — is to live unintelligently. The perfect one experiences the best and the worst in life with equal detachment because he is ever established in the true and eternal which is the very Self.

Arjuna had asked Lord Krishna how a perfect master speaks, and this stanza may be considered as an answer to it. Since the perfect person of wisdom neither feels any aversion for the sorrows nor rejoices at the joys of life, he neither compliments anything in the world, nor does he condemn anything. To him everything is wonderful. He sees things as they are, uncolored by his own mental moods. Such a perfect one is beyond all the known principles of behaviorism of Western psychology.

After explaining that a perfect one is (a) ever satisfied in the Self, (b) that he lives in perfect equanimity in pleasure and pain, and (c) that he has a complete absence of attachment to rejoicing and aversion, the following verse points out how a man of steady wisdom, has the special knack of withdrawing his senses from all the disturbing fields of objects.

> When like the tortoise, which withdraws all its limbs, he can withdraw his senses from the sense objects, then his wisdom becomes steady. (II:58)

The simile of the tortoise used here is very effective. Just as a tortoise can instinctively withdraw all its limbs into itself even at the most distant suggestions of danger and feel safe within itself.

In the same way, a person of steady wisdom is capable of so withdrawing himself that he does not contact the objects through the sense organs. This idea is very figuratively demonstrated in the *Praśna Upaniṣad* (II:4) that the Light of Consciousness, as it were, beams out through the seven holes in the cranium, each special beam illuminating only one specific type of object. Thus, the light that passes through the eyes is capable of illuminating only the forms and colors while that which emerges through the ears illumines sound. In the material world we can take the example of the electric light that comes through an ordinary bulb illuminating the objects in the room, while the light emerging from the x-ray penetrates through the form and illumines things that are ordinarily not visible to the naked eye.

In each of us five distinct beams of the same awareness flow out like antennae and they give us complete knowledge of the external world. These five avenues bring to us the innumerable stimuli from the outer world which, reaching the mind, provide all the disturbances that we feel in life. If I am blind, the beauty that I am passing by cannot disturb my mind; if I am deaf, I cannot overhear criticism against me and, naturally, it cannot reach to agitate my mind! The not yet tasted, not yet smelt or the unfelt sense objects can never bring me any sorrow.

Here Krishna reassures Arjuna that a man of steady wisdom is he who has the capacity to fold back his senses from all the fields of their activity. This capacity in an individual to withdraw his senses at will from the fields of objects is called in the *Yoga Śāstra* as *pratyāhāra,* which the yogi accomplishes through control of breath (*praṇāyāma*). To a devotee this comes automatically because he is all eyes and ears only for the form and stories of his beloved Lord. To the student of Vedanta, this *uparati* comes out of a well-developed and sharpened discriminative faculty, by which his intellect makes his mind understand the futility of its going after the sense objects, for his real nature is Infinite Bliss.

Transcending the Ego

Shankara considers the following stanza as an answer that the Lord gives to a possible doubt in Arjuna's mind. "Now, even the senses of a man who is ill, and consequently not able to partake of the sensuous objects, are seemingly under control, but the taste for them does not thereby cease to exist. How does even the taste for sense objects finally end?" Listen:

> The objects of the senses turn away from the abstinent man leaving the longing behind; but his longing also turns away on seeing the Supreme. (II:59)

Without *pratyāhāra* or *uparati* we can observe cases wherein an individual comes to maintain sense withdrawal from the sense objects due to some physical incapacity or due to some special mental mood of temporary sorrow. In all those cases the sense organs come to feel an aversion for their respective objects for the time being, but their inclinations for these objects are lying somewhere dormant. Similarly, Arjuna questions that even in a yogi the capacity to withdraw from the sense world is also temporary and that under favorable or sufficiently tempting circumstances, it may again arise. This doubt is answered here.

From an abstinent person, the sense objects get no doubt repelled. If we observe the flight of the objects of sensuousness from the shops to their customers, we can understand this point very clearly. They always reach only those who are courting them and who want to posses them. Artists, doctors, or lawyers do not purchase ploughs, but they must necessarily reach the homes of the farmers. Similarly, all sense objects ultimately reach to serve those who are courting them with burning desires. From one who is completely abstinent, sense objects must necessarily become repelled.

But even though the sense objects may temporarily seem to turn away from one who is abstinent, the deep taste for these sense objects ingrained in the mind of the seeker is very difficult to erase completely. Krishna in his supreme wisdom assures the seeker that all those mental impressions of sensuousness lived in the past by the ego from the beginningless past will be totally erased or at least made ineffective — like roasted seeds — when the seeker transcends the ego and comes to experience the Self.

And this is not very difficult to understand since we know that the objects of sorrow and the occasions of tragedy in one plane of consciousness are not available in another plane of awareness. The kingship that I enjoy in my dream does not add anything to my dignity when I wake up to realize my insignificant existence. Conversely, my meager existence in the waking state will not debar me from the kingly glory in my dream kingdom! Similarly, the ego, which exists now through the waking, dream, and deep-sleep states, has gathered to itself many impressions, all of them purely sensuous. But these cannot be effective when the same ego, transcending these three planes, comes to experience the plane of God-consciousness. He who would acquire steadiness of right Knowledge (*prajña*) should bring the senses under control. For, if not controlled, they will do harm. So, the Lord says:

> The turbulent senses O son of Kunti, do violently carry away
> the mind of a wise man though he be striving to control them.
> (II:60)

So far the Lord has emphasized that a perfect master is one who has complete control over his senses. In India a mere philosophical idea in itself is not considered anything more than a poetic ideology, and it is not accepted as a spiritual thesis unless it is a complete technique by which the seeker can come to *live* that philosophy in his own subjective experience. True to this traditional faith, here, in the *Bhagavad Gītā*, the Lord is indicating to Arjuna the practical methods by which he can attempt to reach the eminence of perfection found in all men of steady wisdom.

The ignorance of the spiritual Reality functions in an individual in three distinct ways. These three are called the *guṇa*:

un-activity (*sattva*), activity (*rajas*); and inactivity (*tamas*). [See *Bhagavad Gītā* Chapter XIV for a complete study of the *Guṇa*.] The psychological being in everyone comes under the influence of three different climatic conditions. They influence the mental and the intellectual caliber of every individual, and provide the distinct flavor in each personality. All three are always present in everyone, but their proportion differs slightly from person to person; hence, the distinct aroma in the character and behavior of each individual. Unless these are well controlled, they will drag the mind to the field of the sense objects and thus create a chaotic condition within, which is experienced as sorrow.

Lord Krishna asserts in the above stanza that "This happens even to a highly evolved seeker." With this assertion he is warning the seeker in Arjuna that he should not, on any score, let his objective mind take hold of and enslave his subjective intellectual personality. This warning is quite appropriate and timely in the scheme of thought in this chapter.

Invariably, among those who are practicing religion, the common cause by which many true seekers fall from the path is the same all over the world. After a few years of practice, they will no doubt come to live a certain inexplicable inward joy and over-confident they often become vain of their progress and relax in their austerities, *tapas*. Once the individual goes back to the field of the senses, the turbulent senses violently snatch the mind away from the poise of its perfect meditation.

Steadfast in Wisdom

Having restrained them all, he should sit steadfast, intent on Me; his wisdom is steady whose senses are under control. (II:61)

Since the sense organs are thus the saboteurs in the kingdom of the spirit who bring a disastrous downfall to the empire of the soul, Arjuna is warned here that as a seeker of Self-perfection he should constantly strive to control all his sense organs and their lustful wanderings into their respective fields. Modern psychology certainly would look down upon this *Bhagavad Gītā* theory because, according to Freud and others, sensuousness is instinctive in man and according to them, to control is to suppress, and no science of mental life can accept that suppression is psychologically healthy. But the Vedic teaching is not pointing to any mental suppression at all. They are only advising an inward blossoming, an inner growth and development, by which its earlier fields of enjoyments through the senses drop out of the fuller grown man who has come to the perception of a newer field of ampler joys and more satisfying bliss.

The idea is very well brought out here in the stanza when Lord Krishna, as though in the very same breath, repeats both the negative and the positive aspects of the technique of self-development. He advises not only a withdrawal from unhealthy sensuousness but also gives the healthy method of doing so by explaining to us the positive technique in Self-perfection. Through a constant attempt at focusing our attention "On Me, the Supreme," he advises the disciples to sit steady.

In this simple-looking statement of half-a-stanza, the *Bhagavad Gītā* explains the entire technique of Self-development. Immoral impulses and unethical instincts that bring a person down to the level of a mere brute are the result of endless lives spent among sense objects during the infinite number of different manifestations through which the embodied soul — the ego — in each one of us had previously passed. The thick coating of mental impressions thus gathered is humanly impossible for one solitary individual to erase or transcend in one's short lifetime. Naturally, this is the despair of all the promoters of ethics, the teachers of morality and the masters of spirituality. The ancient rishis, in their lived experience, discovered for themselves a technique by which all these mental tendencies can be eradicated. To expose the mind to the quiet atmosphere of meditation upon the all-perfect Being is to heal the mind of its ulcers. He who has come to gain a complete mastery over his sense organs by this process is called the one who is steadfast in wisdom.

The concealed suggestion in the stanza is quite obvious: no one who with excessive force and by the sheer strength of will controls his sense organs has any chance of flowering into full-blown spiritual beauty. When the sense organs, of their own accord, have come back tamely to lie surrendered at the feet of one who has rediscovered the infinite perfection in himself, he is called a Man of Perfection. He has neither ruined his instruments of cognition nor has he closed down the arches of knowledge in him. A perfect one is he whose sway over the animal in him is so complete that the inner Satan has become, for the sage in him, a tamed animal to run errands and to serve him faithfully.

XI

My Master

by Sogyal Rinpoche

I was born in Tibet and I was six months old when I entered the monastery of my master Jamyang Khyentse Chökyi Lodrö, in the province of Kham. In Tibet we have a unique tradition of finding the reincarnations of great masters who have passed away. They are chosen young and given a special education to train them to become the teachers of the future. I was given the name Sogyal, even though it was only later that my master recognized me as the incarnation of Tertön Sogyal, a renowned mystic who was one of his own teachers and a master of the Thirteenth Dalai Lama.

My master, Jamyang Khyentse, was tall for a Tibetan, and he always seemed to stand a good head above others in a crowd. He had silver hair, cut very short, and kind eyes that glowed with humor. His ears were long, like those of the Buddha. But what you noticed most about him was his presence. His glance and bearing told you that he was a wise and holy man. He had a rich, deep, enchanting voice, and when he taught his head would tilt slightly backward and the teaching would flow from him in a stream of eloquence and poetry. And for all the respect and even awe he commanded, there was humility in everything he did.

Jamyang Khyentse is the ground of my life and the inspiration of this book [*The Tibetan Book of Living and Dying*]. He was the incarnation of a master who had transformed the practice of Buddhism in our country. In Tibet it was never enough simply to have the name of an incarnation, you always had to earn respect, through your learning and through your spiritual practice. My master spent years in retreat, and many miraculous stories are told about him. He had profound knowledge and spiritual realization, and I came to discover that he was like an encyclopedia of wisdom, and knew the answer to any question you might ask him. There were many spiritual traditions in Tibet, but Jamyang Khyentse was acclaimed as the authority on them all. He was, for everyone who knew or heard about him, the embodiment of Tibetan Buddhism, a living proof of how someone who had realized the teachings and completed their practice would be.

I have heard that my master said that I would help continue his work, and certainly he always treated me like his own son. I feel that what I have been able to achieve now in my work, and the audience I have been able to reach, is a ripening of the blessing he gave me.

Childhood Memories

All my earliest memories are of him. He was the environment in which I grew up, and his influence dominated my childhood. He was like a father to me. He would grant me anything I asked. His spiritual consort, Khandro Tsering Chödrön, who is also my aunt, used to say: "Don't disturb Rinpoche, he might be busy,"[1] but I would always want to be there next to him, and he was happy to have me with him. I would pester him with questions all the time, and he always answered me patiently. I was a naughty child; none of my tutors were able to discipline me. Whenever they tried to beat me, I would run to my master and climb up behind him, where no one would dare to go. Crouching there, I felt proud and pleased with myself; he would just laugh. Then one day, without my knowledge, my tutor pleaded with him, explaining that for my own benefit this could not go on. The next time I fled to hide, my tutor came into the room, did three prostrations to my master, and dragged me out. I remember thinking, as I was hauled out of the room, how strange it was that he did not seem to be afraid of my master.

Jamyang Khyentse used to live in the room where his previous incarnation had seen his visions and launched the renaissance of culture and spirituality that swept through eastern Tibet in the last century. It was a wonderful room, not particularly large but with a magical atmosphere, full of sacred objects, paintings, and books. They called it "the heaven of the Buddhas," "the room of empowerment," and if there is one place that I remember in Tibet, it is that room. My master sat on a low seat made of wood and strips of leather and I sat next to him. I would refuse to eat if it was not from his bowl. In the small bedroom close by, there was a veranda, but it was always quite dark, and there was always a kettle with tea bubbling away on a little stove in the corner.

Usually I slept next to my master, on a small bed at the foot of his own. One sound I shall never forget is the clicking of the beads of his *mālā*, his Buddhist rosary, as he whispered his prayers. When I went to sleep he would be there, sitting and practicing; and when I awoke in the morning he would already be awake and sitting and practicing again, overflowing with blessing and power. As I opened my eyes and saw him, I would be filled with a warm and cozy happiness. He had such an air of peace about him.

As I grew older, Jamyang Khyentse would make me preside over ceremonies, while he took the part of chant leader. I was witness to all the teachings and initiations that he gave to others; but rather than the details, what I remember now is the atmosphere. For me he was the Buddha of that there was no question in my mind. And everyone else recognized it as well. When he gave initiations, his disciples were so overawed they hardly dared look into his face. Some would see him actually in the form of his predecessor, or as different buddhas and *bodhisattvas*.[2] Everyone called him *Rinpoche*, "the Precious One," which is the title given to a master, and when he was present no other teacher would be addressed in that way. His presence was so impressive that many affectionately called him "the Primordial Buddha."[3]

Had I not met my master Jamyang Khyentse, I know I would have been an entirely different person. With his warmth, wisdom, and compassion, he personified the sacred truth of the teachings and so made them practical and vibrant with life. Whenever I share that atmosphere of my master with others, they can sense the same profound feeling it aroused in me. What then did Jamyang Khyentse inspire in me? An unshakable confidence in the teachings, and a conviction in the central and dramatic importance of the master. Whatever understanding I have, I know I owe it to him. This is something I can never repay, but I can pass on to others.

Throughout my youth in Tibet I saw the kind of love Jamyang Khyentse used to radiate in the community, especially in guiding the dying and the dead. A lama in Tibet was not only a spiritual teacher but also wise man, therapist, parish priest, doctor, and spiritual healer, helping the sick and the dying. Later I was to learn the specific techniques for guiding the dying and the dead from the teachings connected with the *Tibetan Book of the Dead*. But the greatest lessons I ever learned about death — and life — came from watching my master as he guided dying people with infinite compassion, wisdom, and understanding.

FOOTNOTE

[1]   Rinpoche, a term of respect meaning "Precious One," is given to highly revered teachers in Tibet. It was widely used in the central part of the country; but in eastern Tibet the title was held in such esteem that it tended to be applied only to the greatest masters.

[2]   A *bodhisattva* is a being whose sole wish is to benefit all sentient beings, and who therefore dedicates his or her entire life, work, and spiritual practice to the attainment of enlightenment, in order to be of the greatest possible help to other beings.

3   Jamyang Khyentse was also a leader, one who inspired movements of spiritual change; in everything he did, he promoted harmony and unity. He supported monasteries when they fell on hard times; he discovered unknown practitioners of great spiritual attainment; and he encouraged masters of little-known lineage, giving them his backing so they were recognized in the community. He had great magnetism and was like a living spiritual center in himself. Whenever there was a project that needed accomplishing, he attracted the best experts and craftsmen to work on it. From kings and princes down to the simplest person, he gave everyone his unstinting personal attention. There was no one who met him who did not have their own story to tell about him.

XII

My Guru: Shri Yukteswar

by Paramahansa Yogananda

Shri Yukteswar's mother lived in the Rana Mahal district of Banaras where I had first visited my guru. Gracious and kindly, she was yet a woman of very decided opinions. I stood on her balcony one day and watched mother and son talking together. In his quiet, sensible way, Master was trying to convince her about something. He was apparently unsuccessful, for she shook her head with great vigor.

"Nay, nay, my son, go away now! Your wise words are not for me! I am not your disciple!"

Shri Yukteswar backed away without further argument, like a scolded child. I was touched at his great respect for his mother even in her unreasonable moods. She saw him only as her little boy, not as a sage. There was a charm about the trifling incident; it supplied a sidelight on my guru's unusual nature, inwardly humble and outwardly unbendable.

The monastic regulations do not permit a swami to retain connection with worldly ties after their formal severance. He may not perform the ceremonial family rites that are obligatory on the householder. Yet Shankara, reorganizer of the ancient Swami Order, disregarded the injunctions. After the death of his beloved mother, he cremated her body with heavenly fire that he caused to spurt from his upraised hand.

Shri Yukteswar also ignored the restrictions — in a fashion less spectacular. When his mother passed on, he arranged for crematory services by the holy Ganges in Banaras and fed many Brahmins, in conformance with householder customs.

The *śāstrika* prohibitions were intended to help swamis to overcome narrow identifications. Shankara and Shri Yukteswar had wholly merged their being in the impersonal Spirit; they needed no rescue by rule. Sometimes, too, a master purposely ignores a canon in order to uphold its principle as superior to and independent of form. Thus Jesus plucked ears of corn on the day of rest. To the inevitable critics he said: "The Sabbath was made for man, and not man for the Sabbath." (Mark II:27)

With the exception of the scriptures, Shri Yuhkteswar read little. Yet he was invariably acquainted with the latest scientific discoveries and other advancements of knowledge. A brilliant conversationalist, he enjoyed an exchange of views on countless topics with his guests. My guru's ready wit and rollicking laugh enlivened every discussion. Often grave, master was never gloomy. "To seek the Lord, men need not 'disfigure their faces,'" he would say, quoting from the Bible (Matthew VI:16). "Remember that finding God will mean the funeral of all sorrows."

Among the philosophers, professors, lawyers, and scientists who came to the hermitage, a number arrived for their first visit with the thought of meeting an orthodox religionist. Occasionally a supercilious smile or a glance of amused tolerance would betray that the newcomers expected nothing more than a few pious platitudes. After talking with Shri Yukteswar and discovering that he possessed precise insight into their specialized fields of knowledge, the visitors would part reluctantly.

My guru ordinarily was gentle and affable to guests; his welcome was given with charming cordiality. Yet inveterate egotists sometimes suffered an invigorating shock. They confronted in Master either a frigid indifference or a formidable opposition: ice or iron!

Assimilating the Knowledge

A noted chemist once crossed swords with Shri Yukteswar. The visitor would not admit the existence of God, inasmuch as science has devised no means of detecting Him.

"So you have inexplicably failed to isolate the Supreme Power in your test tubes!" Master's gaze was stern. "I recommend a new experiment; examine your thoughts unremittingly for twenty-four hours. Then wonder no longer at God's absence."

A celebrated scholar received a similar jolt. It came during his first visit to the ashram. The rafters resounded as the guest recited passages from the *Mahābhārata*, the Upanishads, and *bhāṣaya* (commentaries of Shankara).

"I am waiting to hear you." Shri Yukteswar's tone was inquiring, as though silence had reigned. The pundit was puzzled.

"Quotations there have been, in superabundance," Master's words convulsed me with mirth, as I squatted in my corner at a respectful distance from the visitor. "But what original commentary can you supply, from the uniqueness of your particular life? What holy text have you absorbed and made your own? In what ways have these timeless truths renovated your nature? Are you content to be a hollow tape-recorder, mechanically repeating the words of other men?"

"I give up!" the scholar's chagrin was comical. "I have no inner realization."

For the first time, perhaps, he understood that discerning placement of a *comma* does not atone for a spiritual *coma*.

"These bloodless pedants smell unduly of the lamp," my guru remarked after the departure of the chastened one. "They consider philosophy to be a gentle intellectual setting-up exercise. Their elevated thoughts are carefully unrelated either to the crudity of outward action or to any scourging inner discipline!"

Master stressed on other occasions the futility of mere book learning.

"Do not confuse understanding with a larger vocabulary," he remarked. "Sacred writings are beneficial in stimulating desire for inward realization, if one stanza at a time is slowly assimilated. Otherwise, continual intellectual study may result in vanity, false satisfaction, and undigested knowledge."

Shri Yukteswar related one of his own experiences in scriptural edification. The scene was a forest hermitage in eastern Bengal, where he observed the procedure of a renowned teacher, Dabru Ballav. His method, at once simple and difficult, was common in ancient India.

Dabru Ballav had gathered his disciples around him in the sylvan solitude. The holy *Bhagavad Gītā* was open before them. Steadfastly they looked at one passage for half an hour, then closed their eyes. Another half-hour slipped away. The master gave a brief comment. Motionless, they meditated again for an hour. Finally, the guru spoke.

"Do you now understand the stanza?"

"Yes, sir." One in the group ventured this assertion.

"No, not fully. Seek the spiritual vitality that has given these words the power to rejuvenate India century after century." Another hour passed in silence. The master dismissed the students, and turned to Shri Yukteswar. "Do you know the *Bhagavad Gītā*?"

"No, sir, not really; though my eyes and mind have run through its pages many times."

"Hundreds have replied to me differently!" The great sage smiled at Master in blessing. "If one busies himself with an outer display of scriptural wealth, what time is left for silent inward diving after the priceless pearls?"

Shri Yukteswar directed the study of his own disciples by the same intensive method of one-pointedness. "Wisdom is not assimilated with the eyes, but with the atoms," he said. "When your conviction of a truth is not merely in your brain but in your being, you may diffidently vouch for its meaning." He discouraged any tendency a student might have to consider book knowledge a necessary step to spiritual realization.

"The rishis wrote in one sentence profundities that commentating scholars busy themselves over for generations," he said. "Endless controversy is for sluggard minds. What more quickly liberating thought than 'God is' — nay, 'God'?"

Returning to Simplicity

But man does not easily return to simplicity. It is seldom "God" for an intellectualist, but rather learned pomposity. His ego is pleased that he can grasp such erudition.

Men who were pride-fully conscious of their wealth or worldly position were likely, in Master's presence, to add humility to their other possessions. On one occasion a local magistrate requested an interview at the seaside hermitage in Puri. The man, who was reputed to be ruthless, had it well within his power to dispossess us of the ashram. I mentioned this fact to my guru. But he seated himself with an uncompromising air, and did not rise to greet the visitor.

Slightly nervous, I squatted near the door. Shri Yuhkteswar failed to ask me to fetch a chair for the magistrate, who had to be content with a wooden box. There was no fulfillment of the man's obvious expectation that his importance would be ceremoniously acknowledged.

A metaphysical discussion ensued. The guest blundered through misinterpretations of the scriptures. As his accuracy sank, his ire rose.

"Do you know that I stood first in the M.A. examination?" Reason had forsaken him, but he could still shout.

"Mr. Magistrate, you forget that this is not your courtroom," Master replied evenly. "From your childish remarks one would surmise that your college career had been unremarkable. A university degree, in any case, is not related to Vedic realization. Saints are not produced in batches every semester like accountants."

After a stunned silence, the visitor laughed heartily.

"This is my first encounter with a heavenly magistrate," he said. Later he made a formal request, couched in the legal terms that were evidently part and parcel of his being, to be accepted as a "probationary" disciple.

On several occasions Shri Yukteswar, like Lahiri Mahashaya, discouraged "unripe" students who wished to join the Swami Order. "To wear the ochre robe when one lacks God-realization is misleading to society," the two masters said. "Forget the outward symbols of renunciation which may injure you by inducing false pride. Nothing matters except your steady, daily spiritual advancement."

In measuring the worth of a man, a saint employs an invariable criterion, one far different from the shifting yardsticks of the world. Humanity — so variegated in its own eyes — is seen by a master to be divided into only two classes: ignorant men who are not seeking God, and wise men who are.

XIII

Bishrul Hafi: A Rare Soul

by *Susunaga Weeraperuma*

Bishrul Hafi is an unconventional Shri Lankan Muslim descended from Arab settlers on the island. One of his ancestors was a saint named Hajiar Appa. He is a rare soul and considered a Sufi mystic.

Once a businessman, he experienced an inward transformation in his late thirties. He began leading a contemplative life and spent much of his time in the solitude of his rubber-estate bungalow. There he prayed to Allah.

"During the seven years I lived on the estate," he recalls, "I purified my heart. I didn't care for clothes. I don't care what others call me. I only care about what my Creator calls me."

Hafi is now a Justice of the Peace. He shuns all publicity and loves his quiet life in a rural hamlet about twenty miles from Colombo. Although considered by others as a man of God. Hafi has no such estimation about himself. He regards himself as nothing more than an ordinary person. A visitor once exclaimed, "What a great mystic you are!" To this Hafi replied, " I am not of any importance. I am not even a speck of dust in the universe. Only the Creator matters, not me, and I am unworthy of Him."

The following incident from his life would reveal his reverence for the traditions of other religions: One evening Hafi was reading from the *Dhammapāda*, the great Buddhist classic. He was wide-awake. He noticed that his subtle body was being lifted out of its physical frame. It soared higher and higher until he had a vivid vision of the Buddha in a blessing pose. Hafi said that it was the most ecstatic of all his spiritual experiences. When he mentioned this to a group of Buddhist monks, they expressed amazement. They could understand his having experiences in the Islamic tradition but not in the Buddhist one. Thereupon Hafi quoted from Prophet Mohammed who had enjoined Muslims to revere all prophets.

Hafi is a good conversationalist with a fine command of English. Ask him a question and words of wisdom flow from his lips. It is not unusual for him, in the midst of a solemn discussion, to crack jokes or relate stories. From time to time serious seekers call on him to discuss spiritual matters.

The writer has had the privilege of sitting and talking to Hafi for hours. The following are excerpts from such conversations during the visit of the writer to Shri Lanka in 1994:

Question: What is the best spiritual practice?

Hafi: Any vehicle is good — Buddhism, Christianity, Hinduism, Islam or any other religion. If you have an open mind you will naturally venerate all religions. Skip all the rituals. Take the essence of religions and practice it. But keep quiet about your spiritual practices. Do not talk about them. It is like the marital relationship of a couple that is private.

Q: Why is there no spiritual unfoldment despite our performing spiritual practices?

H: The enemy of spiritually is vanity. I think it was Shri Ramakrishna who said that the greatest vanity is the vanity of the saint.

Q: You set great store by spiritual practice. Which do you prefer: meditation, prayer, or social service?

H: All three are enticing.

Q: Do you advocate self-reliance in spiritual matters?

H: You were born alone and you will die alone. You are an individual. Don't be a monkey. You are responsible for your own actions. Your troubles are of your own making. Therefore be your own teacher and do not follow anyone. Develop your uniqueness and find your own path to God. If you depend on others to direct your spiritual path, isn't that like having a wet nurse throughout your life?

Q: What are your views on dreams?

H: Sleep is the half-brother of death. If one overeats, the mind is prone to nightmares. If one has failed to eat enough and is therefore hungry, sound sleep becomes difficult. Avoiding both extremes, eat moderately. Then there is a possibility of having visions and prophetic dreams.

Q: How does one deal with someone who is evil?

H: Don't have anything to do with him. Your only friend in this world is your maker. Therefore, realize the God who dwells within you. Remember the Islamic saying: "If you take one step towards me, I shall take ten steps towards you." You have no real friend except God.

Q: What is your attitude to suffering?

H. Great attainments become possible only through suffering. When you suffer don't try to avoid it but endure suffering with full resignation.

Q: In India there are religious people who concentrate their minds on the primordial sound. Do you approve of this method of meditations?

H: The sound of *Om* is the hum of creation. The sound of this sacred syllable pervades everything. It is this hum that sustains everything. Should this hum cease, the world will also cease. This hum emanated from Him. It is from light that everything came into existence.

Guidelines for Prayer

Q: For you, nothing in life is more important than prayer. Please give a few guidelines.

H.: The whole world is my prayer mat. I pray to God who is everywhere. There is an interval between any two thoughts. It is in this space that creativity is born. During prayer you can widen these intervals. This state is best for praying but you should be fully conscious without falling asleep. Your prayer must be vast. The mind must be unbounded so that you are one with nature. Then, unknowingly, the effects of your prayer will come about.

Realize your powerlessness when praying to the One who is all-powerful. Reduce yourself to nothing. You truly pray when your mind loses its habitual activity and becomes passive. Then the mind is like a piece of cotton wool wafting in the air. That is the ideal state for praying.

There is no particular time or place for praying. One may pray at any time or any place. There are prescribed forms of prayer that one is expected to observe. The Muslim who is required to pray five times a day frequently acts mechanically when he prays. Does he pray with all his mind and heart? Is he not just acting in the way he has been trained? Praying should be a spontaneous act that flows from the very depths of one's being. When praying, one should be totally committed to God. During prayer the ego should be absent and He alone is present in your consciousness.

Mohammed, the Holy Prophet of Islam, used to be in a trance when he prayed. So deep was his trance that immediately after praying he would fail to recognize his wife and children.

All nature is in a prayerful state. The tall trees are praying in a standing posture; the bent trees are bowing in reverence, and creepers are prostrating themselves before him. The bodily postures that a Muslim assumes when he prays are the very same that are observable in nature. All creation prays to the Creator.

Don't force yourself to pray. Engage yourself in prayer only if you are driven by intense devotion to worship the one God.

In life, every action must be regarded as an offering to God. Every action is then a kind of prayer. So your whole life becomes a continuous prayer.

Ask nothing when you pray. If anything is asked at all, then ask God to punish you to the extent that you have asked favors of Him. Submit yourself entirely to Allah and leave it at that. Know that He alone is the Provider. If He gives you nothing, be content with your lot and be just as happy as you would have been if He had given you everything.

XIV

Ramana Maharshi

by Shashi Ahluwalia

Few men can take public adulation in their stride and accept the halo of celebrity without cutting off the umbilical cord, which binds them with the lowest and the lowliest. Some among them consciously eschew the air of superiority, but behind the facade, at times, one can see the ego that craves for exhibition. Only those who have realized the transient nature of praise and the pleasure that goes with it, quell the *aham* (ego) and thus make themselves true friends of the poor and the needy. To this band belongs Maharshi Ramana. His humanism is perceptible in the following incidents:

An old woman named Saubhagyathammal was living in a house near the foot of the Hill. She had made it a daily practice not to take any food until she had *darśan* (vision, sight, beholding a holy person with the wish to receive a blessing) of Bhagavan. She used to come up to Skandashram every day for this purpose. One day Saubhagyathammal did not come. If any of his regular devotees were absent on any particular day Bhagavan never failed to make inquiries and find out the reason. So when the old woman came the next day, he asked her why she did not come on the previous day. She replied: "I had Shri Bhagavan's *darśan* yesterday."

"But you did not come yesterday," said Bhagavan.

She replied, "Bhagavan knew that his humble devotee was too feeble to climb the hill and so he made it possible for her to see him from a place close to her house." She explained that she had seen Bhagavan while he was sitting on the stone and cleaning his teeth and said that she was henceforth going to have his *darśan* everyday in the same way. From that time on Bhagavan made it a practice to sit on that stone for nearly half an hour daily. …

Giving His Grace

Once a visitor came to the ashram and started weeping bitterly, "I am a horrible sinner. For a long time I have been coming to your feet, but there is no change in me. Can I become pure at last? How long am I to wait? When I am here near you I am good for a time. But when I leave this place, I become terrible again. You cannot imagine how bad I can be — hardly a human being. Am I to remain a sinner forever?"

Bhagavan answered, "Why do you come to me? What is there between us that you should come here and weep and cry in front of me?"

The man started moaning and crying even more as if his heart was breaking, "All my hopes of salvation are gone. You were my last refuge and you say you have nothing to do with me! To whom shall I turn now? What am I to do? To whom am I to go?"

Bhagavan watched him for some time and said, "Am I your guru that I should be responsible for your salvation? Have I ever said that I am your master?"

"If you are not my master, then, who is? And who are you, if not my master? You are my guru, you are my guardian angel, you will pity me and release me from my sins!" He started sobbing and crying again.

Bhagavan looked alert and matter-of-fact. "If I am your guru, what are my fees? Surely you should pay me for my services."

"But you won't take anything," cried the visitor, "What can I give you?"

"Did I ever say that I don't take anything? And did you ever ask me what you can give me?"

"If you would take, then ask me; there is nothing I would not give you."

"All right. Now I am asking. Give me. What will you give me?"

"Take anything, all is yours."

"Then give me all the good you have done in this world."

"What good could I have done? I have not a single virtue to my credit."

"You have promised to give. Now give. Don't talk of your credit. Just give away all the good you have done in your past."

"Yes, I shall give, but how does one give? Tell me how the giving is done and I shall give you."

"Say as follows: 'All the good I have done in the past I am giving away entirely to my guru. Henceforth I have no merit from it nor have I any concern with it.' Say it with your whole heart."

"All right, Swami, I am giving away to you all the good I have done so far if I have done any and all its good effects. I am giving it to you gladly, for you are my master and you are asking me to give it all away to you."

"But this is not enough," said Bhagavan sternly.

"I gave you all I have and all you asked me to give. I have nothing more to give."

"No, you have. Give me all your sins."

The man looked wildly at Bhagavan, terror-stricken "You do not know, Swamiji, what you are asking for, if you knew you would not ask me. If you take over my sins, your body will rot and burn. You do not know me, you do not know my sins. Please do not ask me for my sins." And he wept bitterly.

"I shall look after myself, don't you worry about me," said Bhagavan. "All I want from you is your sins."

For a long time the bargain would not go through. The man refused to part with his sins, but Bhagavan was adamant. "Either give me your sins along with your merits, or keep both and don't think of me as your master."

In the end the visitor's scruples broke down and he declared: "Whatever sins I have done, they are no longer mine. All of them and their results, too, belong to Ramana."

Bhagavan seemed to be satisfied, "From now on there is no good nor bad in you. You are just pure. Go and do nothing, neither good nor bad. Remain yourself, remain what you are."

That fortunate visitor was never seen in the ashram again. He might have been in no further need of coming.

The Compassionate One

Once some devotees brought lots of sweets to the ashram and sought permission of Bhagavan to distribute them amongst the people in the hall. Just then an old woman brought with her two or three *dosas* (pancakes) enclosed in a Banyan-leaf bowl. She went straight to Bhagavan and said: "Swami, take these *dosas*, I am sorry, I had nothing better to bring." So saying, she tried to hand them over to Bhagavan directly. People nearby tried to prevent her from doing so by saying, "Please put them somewhere else." She got angry, and all were taken aback by her authoritative attitude.

Bhagavan stretched out his hand and accepted her offerings with the greatest kindness, saying, "Grandma, they are little children who do not know what is what. Please do not take it otherwise. With what flour did you prepare these *dosas*? Are none of your brother's sons looking after you properly? How are you able to maintain yourself? Did you come walking, or in a cart?" Thus inquiring about her welfare, Bhagavan began eating the *dosas*. Even though they were not properly roasted he ate them with great relish as if they were equal to nectar.

The old woman sat there overwhelmed with joy and un-imaginable happiness. Bhagavan afterwards asked for some sweetmeats, took a little of each variety, said that was enough for him and instructed his attendants to distribute the rest amongst themselves and the people there, giving the rest of his share to the old woman. She got up, prostrated before Bhagavan, took her share of the sweetmeats as *prasādam* and left saying, "What does it matter how others look after me, Swami? By your grace I am selling *dosas* and making a living out of the business. It is enough if I could pass the rest of my life thus."

After she left, the attendants asked, "Instead of eating those *dosas* that are not properly roasted, why not give them to us and eat the sweets?"

Bhagavan said, "Oh! Those sweets, you think will be much tastier than these *dosas*? If you want, you eat all the sweets. These *dosas* are enough for me." The attendants could say no more. Bhagavan continued, "Poor old woman, what can she do? She brought what she had. When I was on the hill, she and her husband used to come to me. She used to bring me something to eat now and then. After her husband passed away she lived with her brother. Even he passed away. As her brother's sons did not look after her properly and turned her out, she has been staying somewhere else and has been living by trying to sell *dosas*, it seems. It is she who had a platform constructed near Mother's Samadhi where I used to sit and had it covered by palm leaves. Till then, I used to sit under a tree. 'Aya! Swami is sitting on the floor and is exposed to the sun!' So saying, she got the platform built. It is her brother's son that has repaired Draupadamma's temple. Having grown old, she does not come here often. See how she has come here all this distance, with great effort, helped by the walking stick!" He ate all the *dosas* without leaving even a crumb.

Sympathy for All

His heart reached out in sympathy to all living beings even to animals. This is testified by Arthur Osborne who had lived in the ashram with the Maharshi. To quote him, "He never referred to an animal in the normal Tamil style as 'it' but always as 'he' or 'she.' He would say 'Have the lads been given food?' And it would be the ashram dogs he was referring to. 'Give Lakshmi her rice at once' — and it was the cow Lakshmi that he meant. It was a regular ashram rule at mealtime the dogs were fed first, then any beggars who came, and last the devotees. Knowing Shri Bhagavan's reluctance to accept anything that was not shared by all alike, I was surprised once to see him tasting a mango between meals and then I saw the reason. The mango season was just beginning and he wanted to see whether it was ripe enough to be given to the white peacock that had been sent by the Maharani of Baroda and had become his ward. There were other peacocks also. He would call to them, imitating their cry, and they would come to him and receive peanuts, rice, and mango. On the last day before his physical death, when the doctors said the pain must be frightful, he heard a peacock screech on a nearby tree and asked whether they had received their food.

Squirrels used to hop through the window onto his couch and he would always keep a little tin of peanuts beside him for them. Sometimes he would hand a visiting squirrel the tin and let it help itself, sometimes he would hold out a nut and the little creature would take it from his hand. One day, when, on account of his age and rheumatism, he had begun to walk with the aid of a staff he was descending the few steps from the Hill into the ashram compound when a squirrel ran past his feet, chased by a dog. He called out to the dog and threw his staff between them, and in doing so he slipped and broke his collarbone; but the dog was distracted and the squirrel saved."

The Maharshi would not have snakes killed where he resided. "We have come to their home and have no right to trouble

or disturb them. They do not molest us." And they didn't. Once
he was sitting on the hillside when a snake crawled over his legs.
He neither moved nor showed any alarm. A devotee asked him
what it felt like to have a snake pass over one and, laughing, he
replied, "Cool and soft."

The Maharshi's most favorite animal was a cow named
Lakshmi. When it seemed that her end was near, Bhagavan went
to her "Amma (Mother)," he said, "you want me to be near
you?" He sat down beside her and took her head on his lap. He
gazed into her eyes and placed his hand on her head as though
giving her *dīkṣā* (initiation) and also over her heart. Holding his
cheek against hers, he caressed her. Satisfied that her heart was
pure and free from all *vāsanā* and centered wholly on Bhagavan,
he took leave of her and went to the dining-hall for lunch.
Lakshmi was conscious up to the end; her eyes were calm. At
eleven-thirty at night she died. She was buried in the ashram
compound with full funeral rites, beside the graves of a deer and
a crow, which Shri Bhagavan had also caused to be buried there.
A square stone was placed over her grave mounted by a likeness
of her. On the stone was engraved an epitaph that Shri Bhagavan
had written stating that she had attained *mukti* (liberation).
Devaraja Mudaliar asked Bhagavan whether that was a conven-
tional phrase, as the phrase that someone has attained *samādhī* is
a polite way of saying that he was dead, or whether it really
meant *mukti*, and Shri Bhagavan said that it meant *mukti*.

Once the Maharshi saw somebody cutting a twig in the night
for use the next morning as a toothbrush "Can't you let the tree
sleep in peace? Surely you can have your twig in the daytime.
Why not have a little sense and compassion? A tree does not
howl nor can it bite or run away, but does that mean you can do
anything to it?" Another time somebody was picking a tree to its
last flower. Bhagavan was quite indignant, "Why not leave
some flowers for the poor tree? It likes them, it needs them. You
people pluck the flowers to the last bud as if they were something very precious and then you just let them wither and perish.

On the tree they would live a little longer. I really cannot understand why you are so cruel."

We make a little fuss about a human being, but are quite indifferent to an insect or a tree. To Bhagavan all were equally alive, equally important, he could feel the pain even in a blade of grass.

He was a *jīvanmukta* — free from all mortal bonds. It was this freedom which permeated his reaction to the world around him. With charity for all, with malice toward none, he drew unto himself more and more devotees. The circle widened, but he remained at the core, radiating the light of humanism.

XV

My Guru:
Swami Chinmayananda

by Swamini Saradapriyananda

When I joined the ashram in 1965, Shri Gurudev, Swami Chinmayananda, was conducting a twenty-one day lecture series (*yajña*) in Bombay. Before going to the morning class in the city, Swamiji was teaching *Muṇḍakopaniṣad* to the senior group and we were all allowed to attend it. I was in seventh heaven. After years and years of monotonous work in the office, I was transported to another world where hour after hour, day after day, there was only spiritual study. All those around me had only one theme to talk about — the Upanishad or the jokes cut by Shri Swamiji in the class.

I came to the Bombay *yajña* for the sole purpose of joining the ashram. Though five or six days had passed I was hesitating to broach the subject with Swamiji. I was very emotional at the time and afraid of bursting into tears and making a fool of myself. Swamiji must have sensed it. One morning he was explaining the meaning of a mantra that dealt with *Brahmaloka* in the second chapter of *Bhagavad Gītā*, using the following verse from *Muṇḍaka Upaniṣad* to illustrate his point.

> But they who perform *tapas* and *śraddhā* in the forest, having control over their senses, learned, and living the life of a mendicant, go through the orb of the sun, their good and bad deeds consumed, where the immortal and un-decaying *Puruṣa* is. (I:2.11)

He said, "This is *Brahmaloka*. Now you have come here. You won't go back!" My heart was thrilled with joy, but still I did not dare go to his cottage to make it final. So the next morning in class, while reviewing the previous day's lesson, he said, "You have come for the *yajña* for three weeks. What will happen to you? Will you go back to your office in Hyderabad?" There was a lump in my throat. Go back from this heaven to that stinking drainage again! Never! The next day I met Shri Gurudev at four a.m. in his cottage and sought permission to join as a student. As I had feared, there was much emotion but the purpose was achieved. Gurudev saw how I was nervously meddling with his desk keys while talking with him but he said nothing.

On another occasion, I wished to speak to him about something very personal, but by the time I reached the cottage, someone was already there. Disappointed, I just prostrated and prepared to come away. Swamiji sensed what was on my mind. He joked, "Any lump in the throat to get rid off?" That was exactly what I needed to do. So I smiled shyly, and the other person was sent away.

I asked, "Swamiji, why am I so emotional whenever I meet you?" Swamiji laughed and remarked, "You feel the emotion and are asking me for the reason!" I saw the logic of the remark and left it there. After attending to the main point that I had asked, Swamiji reverted to the question of emotion and said, "Perhaps, you are emotional by nature and very sensitive always."

"No, Swamiji, my friends call me heartless!"

"Oh, then it is your spirit of surrender that makes you so emotional." Swamiji diagnosed.

In those twenty-one days, I could see the way Gurudev was functioning without taking any rest, even for an hour. In the morning he was available for visitors at 4 a.m. in the office. At 5 a.m. there was a class for the senior students on *Muṇḍaka Upaniṣad*. Immediately afterwards, he left for the morning talks in the city, which was more than an hour's drive away. Then he would go for the breakfast *bhikshā* (food offering). At 9 a.m. there was a class in a girl's college on the *Bhagavad Gītā*, chapter twelve. He returned to the ashram at about 2:00 p.m. to teach *Ātma Bodha* to the junior class. Later in the afternoon, at about 4 p.m. he would leave for a discourse in a college. In the evening, at 6 p.m., one could find him sitting in the lecture hall ready to receive the donations of gold ornaments from devotees for the war effort. Those were the days when the Indian army was resisting Chinese aggression. At 6.30 p.m. he would be at the podium thundering away the deep truths of *Sāṁkhya Yoga* found in the second chapter of the *Bhagavad Gītā*. Every night there was a dinner *bhikshā* at some devotee's house. On return he would lie down in the ashram van and reach the ashram at midnight. Even then he would give some instructions to the office people and go to bed ... when? He alone knew! With all this incessant work, at any given time, he appeared fresh and exuberant, as if he had just woken up after hours of rest.

At one point a text known as *Vivekacūḍāmaṇi* was being taken for us. The classes would be intermittent, three or four days in a month at the most. We would get huge doses of *slokas* (verses) daily because the text was extensive and it was important that a topic be finished every time.

When Gurudev would be away traveling to various *yajñas*, all of us would freely write to him about our problems and inner conflicts. We were sure to get a reply by the next mail as soon as our letters reached him. Once I wrote a very long letter about my life in Hyderabad, the problems that I faced, and the wrong steps I had taken knowingly, just to get his opinion. The reply came back. "Got your kind letter. I liked reading every page of it." All my points had been answered.

"My kind letter?" And he liked reading so many pages of my very bad handwriting! I was overwhelmed by the thought that Swamiji could be so very humble in his attitude even to his own students. In a fit of emotion, shedding copious tears. I wrote back, "Swamiji I am not fit to stand within a mile of you. You call my letter 'kind'! You patiently read all the trash I had written and you liked it!" In this manner I expressed myself several times. The next time when he came to the ashram he looked at me and asked with a twinkle. "How is the fever?" Oh, what a joy that was for me!

In 1967, Swamiji was doing a lecture series in Akola and took me along with him for the chanting. It was my first experience to be in such close proximity to Swamiji in a *yajña* and it was quite a revelation to me. One young girl named Lakshmi accompanied us. We were given rooms on the third floor of the guesthouse of the Berar Oil Company.

It was a ten-day lecture series. Swamiji went out for *bhikshā* daily and also for at least one talk on a general topic somewhere. Altogether, four or five times Swamiji had to come up and down the three flights of stairs. Both ways it was a non-stop run by Swamiji for those ten days. And what energy he displayed!

The food was luxurious and full of delicacies. Biscuits accompanied morning coffee. Breakfast would consist of four or five South Indian style dishes, and lunch was always a sumptuous feast. Heavy snacks were offered at the evening tea and again at night *bhikshā* would be lavish. I fell sick within three days. Even the smell of food caused nausea in me. Swamiji did full justice to all the dishes every time. After breakfast he would leisurely continue to sit at the table munching fistfuls of cashew nuts which were in a bowl and converse with the organizers and us. We threw in a word or two but the dialogue was always with Mr. Menon who was the chief organizer. While chewing the cashew nuts Swamiji would say, "Someone take away the bowl from here. Otherwise all of them would disappear into me." It caused us a lot of amusement but I wondered how Swamiji could digest so much food. I understood it only after three years. In 1969, when Jagadeeswara Temple was consecrated, Swamiji had a high fever. Yet he kept a fast for three days before the consecration. I knew then that fasting and feasting were the same for him. Matter went into matter. He had nothing to do with either!

Once the heater as well as the toilet in Swamiji's bathroom was not working. The heater was working where we had our bath, but it was too far for Swamiji to go. It was the month of January and it was very cold. So they asked me to supply hot water in the mornings. Only two small jars were available which were filled by me and supplied early in the morning.

Now that I look back, the water could hardly have been sufficient. It never struck me to ask Swamiji whether he needed more as both Lakshmi and myself were taking cold baths, as was the custom in the ashram. Swamiji could have asked me but he did not say a word. Personal needs never occupied his thoughts! Yet, he was ever mindful of everyone's needs!

In the ashram I had plenty to do, as I was in charge of sending out *Tapovan Prasad* [Chinmaya Mission's monthly magazine]. In Akola as soon as we arrived, we finished our bath and had breakfast. In the evening the *yajña* would commence. What to do with the long hours? Swamiji sat near the table in the huge drawing room and began writing letters. I went onto the terrace and stood there pondering; how helplessly I depended on Swamiji. If he called me for a moment, I went up with joy. If he did not look at me, I was miserable. I knew that the whole day as well as the next ten days of *yajña* would be similar. Would I be able to survive them? I was very restless.

Swamiji was working at the table and yet he was conscious of what I was feeling on the terrace. He knew the reason too. He called me and took out the letters of the Bombay *Guru Dakṣiṇā* envelopes. He went through each one, handing them over to me with instructions on how to reply. Something to do at last! I was asked to keep an account of the letters to be mailed. And it did not stop with this. He asked me to teach English to Lakshmi. I felt amused and asked, "English?" Swamiji nodded and said, "Yes, one hour every day."

All this kept me busy enough, and on the fourth day I analyzed my restlessness. I approached Swamiji and asked him why I was feeling so restless. Swamiji inquired "What are you restless for?"

I replied, "For no reason at all. Nothing is lacking but I am restless."

Then he clarified, "You were very active before coming to the ashram. Now the work is not sufficient for you. So run about."

"Where to?" I asked. Swamiji kept quiet. I understood that I had to discover it for myself as per my capacities. In the ashram there was some work to do, but what more could be done? It got me thinking. As I went on thinking, fine ideas started coming in a pictorial way and I began putting them down on paper. What would be Swamiji's reaction? Would he approve? I was not sure. To find out, I mailed three pieces to Gurudev. I was in great suspense until I received his reply. Swamiji replied as soon as he received my pieces.

"Got your poems. One is sent to *Tapovan Prasad* with a small correction. The second one has gone to Calcutta for the souvenir. Read Tagore and Sorjini Naidu's poems."

Oh, the joy of it! More and more flowed out. I would keep them all copied in sequence until Swamiji came to the ashram and would then hand them over to him in his cottage. He patiently read all of them even though they were in my terrible handwriting. He always encouraged me by a word, look, or a line through the mail. My versification of *Bhaja Govindam sloka* in English was promptly sent to the printers where the text was given for reprint. When it appeared at the end of the text, I was happy. But when I went through the poems, they were anything but perfect. They were raw, contained no rhythm or melody and yet Swamiji included them in his text to give me encouragement. What love!

Though I was very conscious of his great kindness in going through all the poems and getting them printed, the familiarity of taking his love for granted, crept into me. Of course I did not know it then. I sent a new bunch to Swamiji when he was in

Poona and wrote, "I have been sending several poems like this from time to time and taking up much of your time. If I am going beyond my bounds, won't you tell me?" There was no reply nor did I know what happened to the poems sent by me. Perhaps Swamiji thought that he helped me enough. Perhaps it was his way of teaching me a lesson. Whatever it was, I was in suspense. As time passed and Swamiji did not even glance toward me, my sorrow deepened. It became agony. I wondered where I had gone wrong. The poems came out in mournful streams. When should I give them to Swamiji? Swamiji was leaving for his third global tour and the days were drawing near. I felt desperate. To live in heaven along with the Father would be nice and pleasant. But to live with him on earth could sometimes be worse than hell!

To add to my misery, Swamiji fell sick. He had a high fever and developed a backache as well. He kept to his room and no visitors were allowed. Now there was no hope of coming into contact with him. Slowly he recovered and started to receive people who had urgent work. Where was I? I just needed some sign from Swamiji that he was not angry with me. I sent in a poem with a note… "Swamiji this poem is rather too free. I do not know if it should be seen by anyone or not. If you think that it should not be shown to anyone, I shall tear it up. Please instruct."

At last Swamiji relented. He asked for me. He was lying down on the bed. He was not sick anymore, but needed much rest. He was talking and allowed me to ask questions. At the end I asked, "Swamiji we are all getting caught by the happenings that occur all around us and consequently we react. How does the world appear to you? Do you see it as a dream?" He only smiled, for what kind of a reply could he give me? A waker can never explain the nature of a dream to the dreamers. Well, I had already spent half an hour with him without anyone else being present. It was very gratifying to me. When he saw that I was quite content he said, "Hari Om." I got the hint, prostrated, and came away. Even in his pain he was thinking of my needs, ignoring his own rest! Reassured, I sent the entire bunch of poems to him. It bore the covering sentence, "Written in tears but given in smiles."

At the Feet of the Master

Thou bestoweth a smile — a shaft of light flashes in me
Thou speakest a word — a word of wisdom dawns in me
Thou keepest silence — a host of doubts flees in me
Thou gives Thy feet — a sweetness of grace flushes into me!

The veil rolls aside and the door opens.
Faint hesitant light slowly creeps in.
Washed in tears of true repentance and
Purified by the fires of ordeal
The inner shrine glows in delicate tints
And awaits Thee in thrilled anticipation.
Master, grace the hollow of my heart with Thy hallowed form
Infuse into me the light to see and
The strength to walk the righteous path.
Allow me, Master, to wash Thy feet with tears of joy.
And worship with the flower of my mind.

With a bowl in hand full of sweet memories
I came to Thee seeking more. Thou hast emptied the bowl
Of all that it had, depriving me of my all.
With a bowl in hand full of rosy visions
I came to Thee seeking more. Thou hast taken away from
The bowl all that it contained, leaving me devoid of all.
Seated at Thy feet, gaze intent upon Thee,
I stretch my bowl in humility and surrender.
The bowl is bereft of all
Pray, fill it with Thy grace and vision!

The rivers flowing over hills and dales,
Reach the mighty ocean and find their fulfillment.
My thoughts flying over heights and depths,
Reach your blessed feet and find their fulfillment.

XVI

Satsaṅga with Swamini Saradapriyananda

Compiled by the Editors

Swamini Saradapriyananda affectionately referred to as "Amma" attained *mahāsamādhī* on April 17, 2000. At that time Swami Tejomayananda adorned her by saying: "In spiritual life it is very easy to become a scholar by reading, but to be a saint or a *sādhū* is rare indeed. Tulsidas said: 'A saint is a mobile place of pilgrimage by himself.' Amma was like the convergence of Ganga, Yamuna, and Sarasvati at Prayag — a perfect blend of *bhakti*, *karma*, and *jñāna*, respectively. According to *Śrīmad Bhāgavatam*, a *sādhū* is one who endures his or her suffering patiently, but is compassionate toward others' sufferings and sorrow. Amma was a *sādhū*."

She was a true disciple of a perfect master, Swami Chinmayananda. She was an embodiment of self-determination, overcoming all challenges that stood in the way of her spiritual progress and therefore reached the goal that was indicated to her by her Guru. A perfect teacher, an ocean of virtues, she created inspiration in the hearts of multitudes of people. She was also a great scholar and poet. Amma led an extraordinary life of simplicity and service, exuding fiery dynamism, intellectual brilliance, and loving radiance. She founded and developed four major projects (ashram) in Andhra Pradesh, India, to help villagers, orphans and the elderly. Amma continues to be a beacon to us all.

Following are some of her answers to questions asked by her devotees:

Q: Adi Shankara says in *Ātma Bodha* that action is not an antidote to ignorance. Only knowledge can liberate one. Does it contradict the *karma yoga* preached by Lord Krishna in the *Bhagavad Gītā*?

A: Shankara does not contradict the *Bhagavad Gītā* but only clarifies philosophical terms used in the *Bhagavad Gītā* and other scriptures for the sake of a beginner of Vedanta. Please refer to *Bhagavad Gītā* Chapter IV:33, which says, "All types of actions, Arjuna, come to an end in knowledge."

This knowledge is not intellectual, but an actual experience of Self. Once the Self is experienced, the individuality is no more and naturally that person does not crave to get anything from the world. So the action ends. Shankara states the same thing. An action seeks something as a result. All seeking is due to ignorance. By performing an action the ignorance is not eliminated but perpetrated. Hence, it is not an antidote to ignorance. *Karma yoga* as taught in the *Bhagavad Gītā* is the preliminary practice needed to purify the mind. Krishna explains: "Yogins perform actions without attachment for self-purification." (V:11) This is the purpose of *karma yoga*. After the successful performance of *karma yoga*, the seeker becomes fit for *jñāna*, knowledge.

Q: Is meditation *dhyāna gamyam* a noun or a verb? Do we just remain in It as the end all or be all? Is there nothing further?

A: *Gamyam* means that which is to be reached, it is a noun derived from the verb. As long as we are an individual, the *jīva*, we have to meditate and go beyond the world of phenomenon and get merged in It. Until we reach there, it is an effort. Once we reach, we will know that we have always been "That" and never anything else. We will also know that we never made any effort at all to reach it since we have never been away from It.

Thus all the great spiritual teachers confirm what the scriptures declare: There is neither a seeker nor knowledge, no individual or God; no effort nor realization. It has always been One and even now It is the One. No one reached from anywhere. There is no speech at that state of realization to describe It as a verb or a noun. It is!

After you wake up from the dream, what did you achieve? Did you move anywhere? You were on the bed when you went to sleep. You were on the bed while dreaming and you were still on the bed when you woke up.

Q: You said that the one intelligence in all of us is called the Real. The Supreme Intelligence directs the entire cosmos in perfect order in the universe. What is the role of human limited intelligence? Is there a crossing of the barrier? Or is the concept of "That Great God" a creation of man to keep it as the goal so that we can separate ourselves from the body identification in order that some remote control can take over?

A: "That Great God" is not a mere concept created by man to be kept as a goal. If it is a mere concept, how can anything take over the control when you give up the body identification? God is the positive Supreme Intelligence that keeps the universe in perfect order. At present you are one of the creatures, an insignificant helpless being endowed with a limited intelligence bound by time, space, and causation. So are all the living beings around you. All creatures possess the same intelligence within them in different degrees. The sum total of all individual intelligence is the One that sees and uses the objects of the universe. To invite your attention from the individual to the total, great proclamations or *mahā vākya* are given, one of these is *Prajñānāma Brahma* (Consciousness is Brahman). The limited human intelligence has to cross over the individuality and reach the total. The total also is endowed with the conditionings of time and space. At that level the intelligence has to go beyond those final barriers and explode into the Infinite.

Q: The Upanishads, *Brahma Sūtra*, and the *Bhagavad Gītā* are called the spiritual Trinity. I am told that the Upanishads contain mantras; the *Brahma Sūtra* contain *sūtras*, and that the *Bhagavad Gītā* has *śloka*. What is the difference between mantras, *sūtra*, and *śloka*?

A: The three scriptures cater to three different types of students at different levels of understanding. The Upanishads are called *Śruti Prasthāna*. They are meant for highly evolved students who are already introvert. Just by listening to the teacher they can start reflecting, and reach the goal in meditation right away. The teachings are in mantra form, very profound and deep. Mantra means *mananāt trāyate*, that is, by reflection the mantra gives protection. The mantras are very powerful.

Brahma Sutrā are called *Nyāya Prasthāna*. They are meant for rational thinkers who need food for thought. The *sūtra* is an aphorism, which does not even have full sentences. It just suggests and hints. What the *sūtra* suggests, the intellectual has to come to know, either by discussions with other students, or by the long and deep processes of logical thinking. Finally he has to arrive at the correct meaning of the *sūtra*. Until the conclusion tallies with the other conclusions of the other *sūtra* he will have to do mental experimentation, drop the original conclusions, and take up new ones. This is the path of the intellect.

The *Bhagavad Gītā* is the means for people involved in the world who have loves and hates, attachments and aversions, that is, normal people trying to live a normal righteous life. They have forgotten that they have the spark of Divinity within. The *Gītā* sings the song as the reminder. It is called *Smṛti Prasthāna*. It teaches us how to live the normal life remembering our true nature and conforming to the path that leads to the final goal of the Supreme. The *śloka* are metrical verses sung by the Lord within, for the sake of the confused man.

Q: What is *Sat-Cit-Ānanda*? Are we to believe that it is the final goal and our true nature?

A: *Sat* means existence, *Cit* means knowledge, and *Ānanda* means bliss. These terms indicate the pure Existence, Knowledge, and Bliss without any conditions and partitions. They are declared to be the nature of the Supreme Self by the scriptures and also the true nature of man. One must be thoroughly convinced of the correctness of what the scriptures state by one's own reasoning, *yukti*.

Supposing some god appears before you and offers to grant you many boons, or favors. What will be the first one you ask for? Will it not be health, beauty, and long life? But for how long? You would say forever if possible. The next seeking would be to want knowledge, deep knowledge, without a trace of ignorance. That means, absolute Knowledge. If that boon also is given, you will ask for joy, a perfect joy that never ceases and is not dependent on outer circumstances. This is what is known as absolute Bliss.

You want all three: a perpetual, perfect, healthy, youthful existence, a total knowledge without any ignorance, and absolute joy. If these three boons are given to you what more would you seek? Think!

Since you have health, beauty, and youth perpetually, you do not need hospitals, doctors, nurses, cosmetics and beauty parlors. Since you have perfect knowledge, you don't need schools, colleges, universities, lecturers, libraries or books. Since you have absolute joy coming out of you, you don't need objects of enjoyment, cinemas or TVs. In fact you don't require anything from the world. That means the world becomes redundant. It follows that life itself is redundant. Thus you can see your life is fulfilled and salvation comes. Thus you can see how *Sat Cit Ānanda* is declared as the goal of life!

Man now has existence, knowledge, and bliss in a limited way. All he wants is removal of the limitations that come from thinking that he is the body, mind, and intellect. It becomes clear that when the equipment that make us a personality are removed, we are the infinite *Sat Cit Ānanda*. This is our real nature.

About the Authors

Swami Abhedananda

Swami Abhedananda, born on October 2, 1866, was one of the direct disciples of Ramakrishna Paramahansa and the spiritual brother of Swami Vivekananda. His life was intimately bound up with the Vedanta movement in the West. From 1897-1921 he lectured all over North America and Europe. He was appreciated for his profound scholarship, intellectual brilliance, oratorical talents, and noble character. After returning to India in 1921 he established centers at Calcutta and Darjeeling. He attained *mahasamadhi* on September 8, 1939.

Shashi Ahluwalia

Shashi Ahluwalia is married to B.K. Ahluwalia; together they have co-authored the book *Maharshi Ramana* from which the article used here has been taken. (The editors regret not to have any more information available).

Swami Chidananda

Swami Chidananda is the *Acharya* of Sandeepany Sadhanalaya in Mumbai, which is a primary institute of Vedic studies founded by Swami Chinmayananda. At the age of 23 while still a student at the Indian Institute of Technology, Chennai, he was greatly inspired by Swami Chinmayananda. He joined the Chinmaya Mission in 1984 and was taught by Swami Tejomayananda. Swamiji has served

Chinmaya Mission centers in Bangalore, Delhi, Mumbai, and San Jose, California. He is an effective communicator of spiritual ideas in plain and modern-day language.

Swami Chinmayananda

Swami Chinmayananda, the founder of Chinmaya Mission, was a sage and visionary. He toured tirelessly all around the world giving discourses and writing commentaries on the scriptural knowledge of Vedanta, until he left his bodily form in 1993. (See write-up at the end of this book.)

Anthony de Mello

Anthony de Mello, S.J., was the director of the Sadhana Institute of Pastoral Counseling in Poona, India. A member of the Jesuit province of Bombay, he was widely known in English and Spanish-speaking countries for his retreats, workshops, seminars on prayer, and therapy courses — work which he was involved in for over eighteen years around the world. Though he died in the prime of life, after a brief illness in 1987, he leaves a rich legacy of spiritual teaching through his written and recorded words.

Hazrat Inayat Khan

Hazrat Inayat Khan was born in Baroda on July 5th, 1882 into a musical dynasty, as his grandfather was the court musician of the Maharaja of Baroda. He traveled throughout India and became very well known as a court singer and Veena player. While traveling he studied the religious and mystical orders of India and was initiated into the Sufi order. At the age of 28, he left for the West with his brothers and between 1910 and 1920 they performed in the great concert halls of Europe and America, being the first professional group to present Hindustani and Karnatic music to the West. He founded the Sufi Movement and delivered the Sufi message of love, harmony, and beauty, through his lectures.

Professor P. Krishna

P. Krishna, was a professor of Physics at the Benares Hindu University. He is the Rector of the Rajghat Education Centre, Varanasi. He is a Fellow of the Indian National Science Academy, New Delhi, the author of many books and research papers, and has lectured internationally on socio-philosophical topics.

Swami Ranganathananda

Swami Ranganathananda is the President of the Ramakrishna Math and Mission. He was born in 1908 and joined the order at the early age of seventeen. Swami Ranganathananda has been Secretary of the Ramakrishna Mission Institute of Culture, Director of its School of Humanistic and Cultural Studies, and editor of its monthly journal. In 1986 he became the first recipient of the Indira Gandhi Award for National Integration. He has traveled throughout the world enthralling people with his magnificent exposition of India's ageless culture backed by an erudition, which, though firmly rooted in the Indian scriptures, gives due place to the role of science and technology.

ABOUT THE AUTHORS

Sogyal Rinpoche

Sogyal Rinpoche was born in Tibet and raised by one of the most revered spiritual masters of this century, Jamyang Khyentse Chökyi Lodrö. He travels and lectures throughout the world and is the founder and spiritual director of Rigpa, an international network of Buddhist groups and centers.

Swami Satprakashananda

Swami Satprakashananda (1888-1979) was a senior monk of the Ramakrishna Order of India. He was the founder-head of the Vedanta Society of St. Louis, where he lived as a spiritual teacher continuously since 1938. A graduate of the University of Calcutta with literary abilities, and clear understanding, he served nearly three years as associate editor of the monthly journal *Prabuddha Bharata* and later did the pioneering work in establishing the New Delhi Center before coming to the U.S.

Swamini Saradapriyananda

Swamini Saradapriyananda, was one of the first disciples of Swami Chinmayananda. A lawyer from Hyderabad, she gave up everything for a higher calling. She adopted orphans and elderly alike and established one of the biggest socio-economic projects from the grass roots level, now known as Chinmayaranyam. Her life was an extraordinary example of service and simplicity. She has authored several books and also translated some of Swami Chinmayananda's commentaries into Tamil. Swamini "Amma" attained *mahasamadhi* on April 17, 2000 at Tirupati, India.

Swami Tejomayananda

Swami Tejomayananda, the spiritual head of Chinmaya Mission Centers worldwide is fulfilling the vision of Swami Chinmayananda. Swami Tejomayananda has served as Dean, or *ācārya*, of the Sandeepany Institutes of Vedanta, both in India and California. He has written commentaries on scriptural texts, authored a number of books and translated Swami Chinmayananda's commentaries into Hindi. Swami Tejomayananda excels in expounding a wide spectrum of Hindu scriptures. His easy manner and devotional rendering of Vedantic texts has drawn many newcomers into the spiritual fold.

Swami Vivekananda

Swami Vivekananda was the foremost disciple of Ramakrishna Paramahansa. He was the founder of the Ramakrishna Mission. He became famous in the West through his address at the Parliament of Religions in Chicago in 1893 that helped focus the world's attention on the Vedantic teachings.

Susunaga Weeraperuma

Susunuga Weeraperuma is a Sinhalese Buddhist and a doctor of letters who was born in Shri Lanka where he was raised in the Buddhist religion. He writes regularly for the *Mountain Path*.

Pronunciation of Sanskrit Letters

a	(b*u*t)	k	(*s*kate)	t	{*th*ink or	ś	(*sh*ove)
ā	(f*a*ther)	kh	(*K*ate)	th	{*th*ird	ṣ	(bu*sh*el)
i	(*i*t)	g	(*g*ate)	d	{*th*is or	s	(*s*o)
ī	(be*e*t)	gh	(*g*awk)	dh	{*th*ere	h	(*h*um)
u	(s*u*ture)	ṅ	(si*ng*)	n	(*n*umb)	ṁ	(nasaliza-
ū	(p*oo*l)	c	(*ch*unk)	p	(s*p*in)		tion of
ṛ	(*r*ig)	ch	(mat*ch*)	ph	(loo*ph*ole)		preceding
ṝ	(*rrr*ig)	j	(*J*ohn)	b	(bu*n*)		vowel)
ḷ {no		jh	(*j*am)	bh	(ru*b*)	ḥ	(aspira-
{English		ñ	(bu*n*ch)	m	(*m*uch)		tion of
{equiva-		ṭ	(*t*ell)	y	(*young*)		preceding
{lent		ṭh	(*t*ime)	r	(d*r*ama)		vowel)
e	(pl*ay*)	ḍ	(*d*uck)	l	(*l*uck)		
ai	(h*i*gh)	ḍh	(*d*umb)	v	(*w*ile/*v*ile)		
o	(t*oe*)	ṇ	(u*n*der)				
au	(c*ow*)						

Other Chinmaya Publication Series:

THE *Self-Discovery* SERIES

Meditation and Life
by Swami Chinmayananda

Self-Unfoldment
by Swami Chinmayananda

THE *Hindu Culture* SERIES

Hindu Culture: An Introduction
by Swami Tejomayananda

The Sanskrit word *Mananam* means reflection. The *Mananam Series* of books is dedicated to promoting the ageless wisdom of Vedanta, with an emphasis on the unity of all religions. Spiritual teachers from different traditions give us fresh, insightful answers to age-old questions so that we may apply them in a practical way to the dilemmas we all face in life. It is published by Chinmaya Mission West, which was founded by Swami Chinmayananda in 1975. Swami Chinmayananda pursued the spiritual path in the Himalayas, under the guidance of Swami Sivananda and Swami Tapovanam. He is credited with the awakening of India and the rest of the world to the ageless wisdom of Vedanta. He taught the logic of spirituality and emphasized that selfless work, study, and meditation are the cornerstones of spiritual practice. His legacy remains in the form of books, audio and video tapes, schools, social service projects, and Vedanta teachers who now serve their local communities all around the world.